Pupil Book 5B

Series Editor: Peter Clarke

Authors: Elizabeth Jurgensen, Jeanette Mumford, Sandra Roberts

Contents

6-digit numbers

Read, write, order and compare numbers up to 1 000 000 and determine the value of each digit

Challenge 1

1 Write the place value of each digit in these numbers.

a 28 651
b 31 628
c 45 237
d 58 105
e 39 444
f 63 810

Example

24 738 = 20 000 + 4000 + 700 + 30 + 8

2 Choose two of the numbers from Question 1 and write them out in words.

3 Order each set of numbers, smallest to largest.

a 52 761, 39 163, 16 922, 43 811, 53 178, 83 621
b 37 812, 34 823, 31 243, 30 836, 39 264, 35 144
c 28 476, 28 576, 28 097, 28 312, 28 204, 28 599
d 56 983, 65 411, 56 072, 65 308, 56 333, 65 365
e 12 763, 10 673, 13 703, 17 306, 10 763, 12 367
f 78 653, 78 651, 78 659, 78 654, 78 650, 78 655

Challenge 2

1 Write the place value of each digit in these numbers.

a 164 821
b 272 927
c 406 366
d 793 141
e 804 782
f 577 226

Example

365 871 = 300 000 + 60 000 + 5000 + 800 + 70 + 1

2 Choose two of the numbers from Question 1 and write them out in words.

3 Copy these numbers and write a number in each space, still keeping the order.

a 276 100, ______, 285 365, ______, 291 287

b 346 508, ______, 347 000, ______, 347 580

c 208 156, ______, 218 386, ______, 228 541

d 528 387, ______, 528 598, ______, 528 782

e 811 376, ______, 876 361, ______, 904 326

f 989 532, ______, 991 638, ______, 994 762

4 Write the next number.

a 548 623 b 402 387 c 527 659 d 299 653

e 728 699 f 620 285 g 583 399 h 199 999

1 

a Use the number cards to make ten different 6-digit numbers.

b Order your numbers, smallest to largest.

c Choose two of the numbers and write them out in words.

d Partition two of your numbers to show the place value of each digit.

Hint
Organising your numbers in a systematic way will help to check you do not repeat any answers.

Example

427 082 = 400 000 + 20 000 + 7000 + 80 + 2

2 I'm thinking of a number.

- The 1s digit is 5.
- The 10 000s digit is even.
- The 100s digit is lower than 4.
- The 100 000s digit is higher than 7.

What could my number be? Write down eight possible answers.

6-digit counting and rounding (1)

- Count forwards and backwards in steps of 10, 100 and 1000
- Round any number up to 1 000 000 to the nearest 10, 100 and 1000

1 For each number on the number cards, count on or back in the steps given below. Include ten numbers in each number sequence.

a Count on in 10s.

b Count back in 10s.

c Count on in 100s.

d Count back in 100s.

2 For each number on the number cards, round up or down to the amounts given below.

a Round to the nearest 10.

b Round to the nearest 100.

Challenge 2

1 For each number on the number cards, count on or back in the steps given below. Include ten numbers in each number sequence.

a Count back in 10s.

b Count on in 100s.

c Count on in 1000s.

d Count back in 1000s.

2 Write the two multiples of 10 that each number below comes between on either side of the number. Circle the multiple of 10 that the number rounds to.

3 Using the numbers in Question 2, write the two multiples of 100 that each number comes between on either side of the number. Circle the multiple of 100 that the number rounds to.

4 Using the numbers in Question 2, write the two multiples of 1000 that each number comes between on either side of the number. Circle the multiple of 1000 that the number rounds to.

Challenge 3

1 Explain which digits change when counting on and back in 1000s from any 6-digit number.

2 Play this game with a partner.

- One player should choose a 6-digit start number.
- In your heads, both count on in 1000s five times.
- Write down the number you get to. Do you and your partner have the same number? If not, count together out loud to find the right answer.
- Do this ten times, taking turns to choose the start number.

Repeat the steps above, this time counting back in 1000s.

Negative numbers

- Count backwards through 0 with negative numbers
- Interpret negative numbers in context

1 Start at these numbers and count back ten numbers. Record your numbers on a number line if it helps.

a −4	b −9	c −15	d −20
e −34	f −42	g −50	h −63

2 Write the numbers that are 1 more and 1 less than these numbers.

a −17	b −25	c −39	d −47
e −50	f −65	g −77	h −81
i −59	j −86	k −90	l −95

1 Write the number that is 5 less than these numbers.

a −6	b −14	c −21	d −37
e −42	f −49	g 1	h −63
i −57	j 2	k −72	l 4

2 Write the number that is 13 less than these numbers.

a −25	b −34	c −46	d −52
e 4	f −81	g 7	h 10
i −17	j 12	k −55	l 1

3 Read the temperature on each pair of thermometers. How much has the temperature changed by?

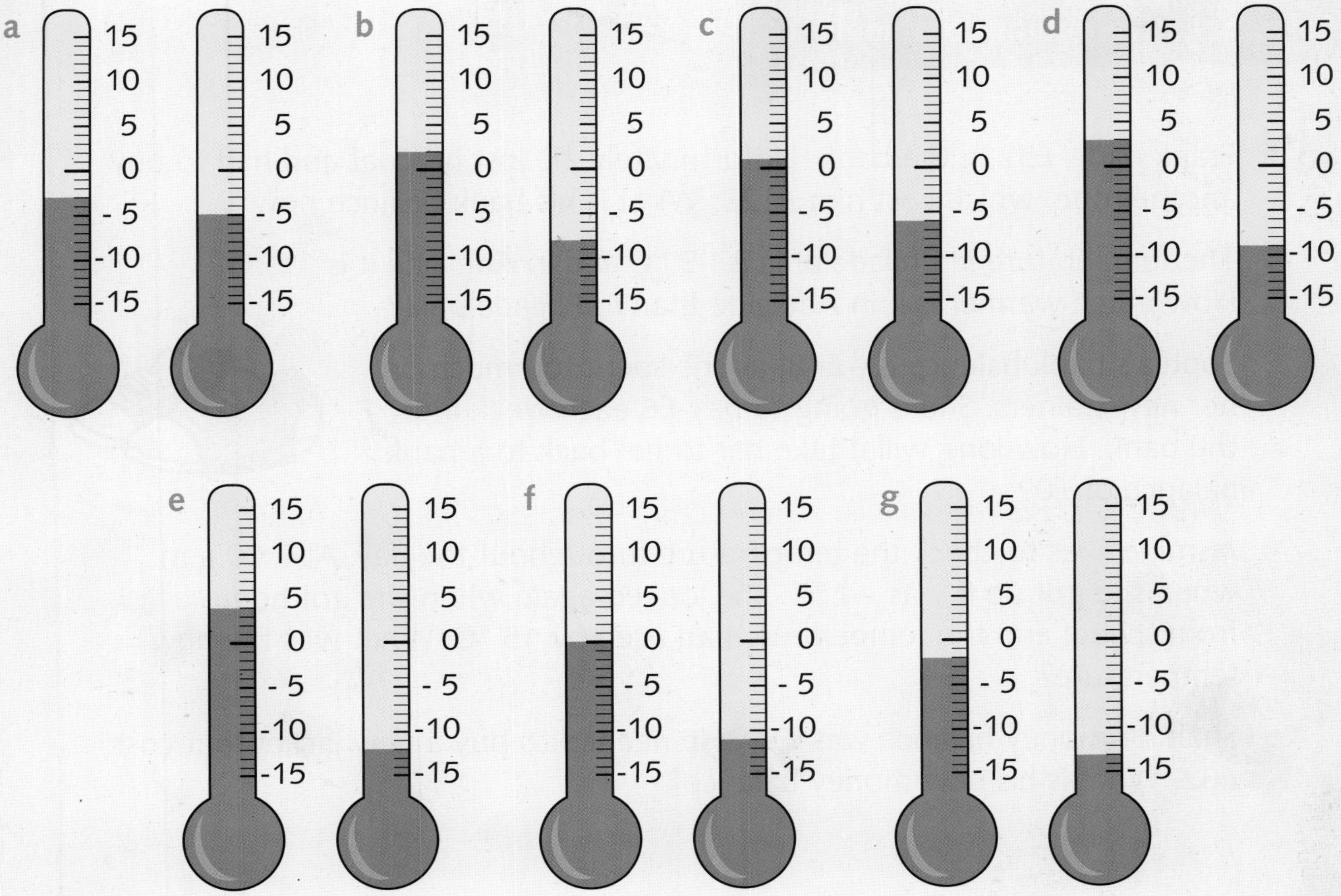

a

b

c

d

e

f

g

Challenge 3

1 Start at these numbers and count back ten times in steps of 3.

a 0 b −4 c −22 d −35 e −47 f −59

g −66 h −86 i −75 j −64 k −91 l −80

2 What would the new temperatures be if it got warmer by 13 °C?

a −16 °C b −25 °C c −34 °C

d −7 °C e −10 °C f −2 °C

Negative problems

Solve negative number problems

1 Frank had –£52 in the bank. Unfortunately, he lost his coat and had to buy another one, which cost him £128. What is his bank balance now?

2 The temperature in Philadelphia is –9 °C and in Adelaide it is 19 °C. How much warmer is it in Adelaide than in Philadelphia?

3 Sophia's bank balance is –£48, as she spent too much on her new trainers. She is going to pay £6 each week into the bank. How long will it take her to get back to a bank balance of £0?

4 Jasmine likes to check the temperature throughout the day. At 7:00 a.m. when she got up it was –4 °C. She looked again when she got home from school and the temperature had risen by 15 °C. What was the new temperature?

5 Shahin's money balance was £39. He needed to buy a new jacket that cost £62. What is his new money balance?

1 Jasmine was given £80 for her birthday. She bought a pair of shoes for £59.50 and a pair of jeans for £43.20. What will her bank balance be now?

2 Susie earns £7 a week for her work at the farm. She also gets an allowance of £10 a month from her parents. In January she spent £6.99 on a book, £18.50 on a new jumper and £25.40 on some boots that were in the sale. What is her balance at the end of January?

3 The temperature in Las Vegas is 19 °C and in Quebec it is –31 °C. What is the difference in temperature?

4 Frank had –£56.20 in the bank. Unfortunately, he lost his phone and had to buy another one, which cost him £234.50. What will his bank balance be now?

5 Rosie made some jelly with water that had a temperature of 51 °C. She put it in the freezer to cool but forgot about it and the temperature dropped by 64 °C and it froze. She got it out and by the time she wanted to eat it the temperature had risen by 33 °C. What temperature was the jelly when she ate it?

6 A business is in trouble. Its bank balance is –£3825. It has two payments owed to it: one for £865 and the other for £643. What will the bank balance be once it receives these payments?

Challenge 3

1 On a winter day Frank's thermometer tells him it is –5·6 °C in his garden and a cosy 23·9 °C in his house. How much warmer is his house than his garden?

2 Rosie's mum has £85 left in her bank account. One morning four bills arrive – car tax £77, mobile phone bill £42.83, car repair £257.45 and vet bill £54.27. What will her bank balance be after she has paid all her bills?

3 A business is in trouble. Its bank balance is –£28 429. It needs to pay its workers this month and that is going to cost them £5842. But it does have two payments owed to it: one for £13 164 and the other for £9899. What will the bank balance be after these transactions have been completed?

4 What is the difference between the temperature of most freezers and room temperature? What is meant by 'room temperature'?

5 Where in the world has the hottest temperature right now? And the coldest? What is the difference between the two temperatures?

Subtracting mentally (3)

Subtract numbers mentally

Challenge 1

Subtract these numbers mentally.

a 19 265 – 50
b 18 487 – 300
c 25 761 – 5000
d 29 938 – 600
e 34 528 – 70
f 35 761 – 6000
g 37 417 – 800
h 39 265 – 90
i 43 872 – 4000
j 46 236 – 70
k 48 582 – 600
l 53 387 – 8000

Challenge 2

1 Subtract these numbers mentally.

a 23 497 – 360
b 26 725 – 3400
c 31 872 – 540
d 34 286 – 5100
e 38 721 – 810
f 39 296 – 4300
g 44 187 – 650
h 47 287 – 8100

2 Subtract these numbers mentally.

a 145 738 – 30 000
b 167 498 – 5000
c 189 386 – 100 000
d 254 276 – 7000
e 276 298 – 50 000
f 351 782 – 200 000
g 385 286 – 900
h 427 318 – 300 000

You will need:

- 1–6 dice

3 Work with a partner.

- Choose a 6-digit number greater than 600 000 and both write it down.
- Each choose a different place value: 100 000s, 10 000s, 1000s or 100s.
- Each roll the dice and use the digit rolled to make a number, with the place value you chose.
- Subtract your number from the number you both chose.
- Check each other's calculations.

Do this ten times.

Challenge 3

1 Subtract these numbers mentally.

a 53 652 – 8700
b 57 131 – 8500
c 68 345 – 890
d 75 462 – 6500
e 81 762 – 7900
f 87 438 – 860
g 487 897 – 60 000
h 491 243 – 200 000
i 523 297 – 8000
j 629 026 – 30 000
k 657 382 – 400 000
l 683 621 – 90 000

2 Use mental methods to find the missing numbers.

a 53 823 – ☆ = 53 473
b 58 762 – ☆ = 52 862
c 64 381 – ☆ = 63 641
d 79 268 – ☆ = 72 868
e 83 726 – ☆ = 76 526
f 92 467 – ☆ = 91 737
g 376 878 – ☆ = 336 878
h 445 983 – ☆ = 437 983
i 482 531 – ☆ = 182 531
j 578 357 – ☆ = 518 357
k 621 788 – ☆ = 616 788
l 685 821 – ☆ = 635 821

Written subtraction (1)

- Subtract whole numbers with 5 digits using the formal written method
- Estimate the answer to a calculation

Challenge 1

First estimate then calculate the answers to these calculations.

a 4256 – 1523
b 5387 – 2159
c 5863 – 3581
d 6278 – 2753
e 7259 – 4076
f 7429 – 3864
g 7382 – 2537
h 8276 – 5928
i 8747 – 1689
j 9065 – 3217
k 7258 – 3419
l 8136 – 2742

Example

6398 – 2519 → 6400 – 2500 = 3900

$$\begin{array}{r} \overset{5}{\cancel{6}}\ \overset{13}{\cancel{3}}\ \overset{8}{\cancel{9}}\ \overset{18}{\cancel{8}} \\ -\ 2\ \ 5\ \ 1\ \ 9 \\ \hline 3\ \ 8\ \ 7\ \ 9 \\ \hline \end{array}$$

Challenge 2

1 First estimate then calculate the answers to these calculations.

Example

45 218 – 27 185 → 45 200 – 27 200 = 18 000

$$\begin{array}{r} \overset{3}{\cancel{4}}\ \overset{15}{\cancel{5}}\ \ \overset{1}{\cancel{2}}\ \overset{11}{\cancel{1}}\ 8 \\ -\ 2\ \ 7\ \ \ 1\ \ 8\ \ 5 \\ \hline 1\ \ 8\ \ \ 0\ \ 3\ \ 3 \\ \hline \end{array}$$

a 18 387 – 12 598
b 25 659 – 17 861
c 27 625 – 21 862
d 37 472 – 29 185
e 46 203 – 32 571
f 53 872 – 28 326
g 57 463 – 25 729
h 68 375 – 42 738
i 70 635 – 51 287
j 73 846 – 48 180
k 75 285 – 38 421
l 81 463 – 46 182

2 Explain how you decide whether to use the written method or a mental method.

3 Work out the missing numbers in these calculations.

a

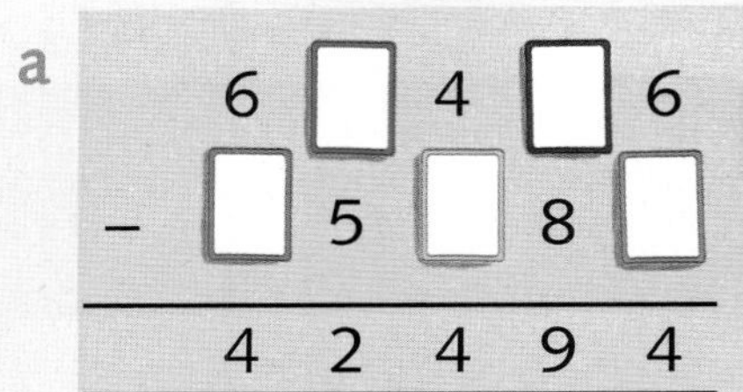

b

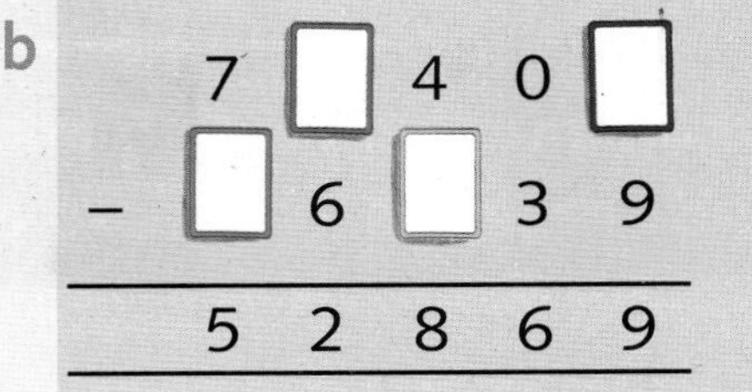

4 Make up a missing number calculation for a partner. Remember to check that it can be worked out.

Challenge 3

1 First estimate then calculate the answers to these calculations.

Example

63 296 – 29 537 → 63 300 – 29 500 = 33 800

```
   5  12   12  8  16
   6  3    2   9  6
 – 2  9    5   3  7
   3  3    7   5  9
```

a 26 836 – 17 358 b 38 375 – 23 596 c 42 487 – 27 609

d 53 272 – 36 085 e 59 351 – 25 682 f 63 287 – 35 928

g 67 261 – 42 574 h 75 397 – 49 628 i 80 232 – 51 517

2 How would you work out these calculations?

Shall I use a written or mental method?

a 82 222 – 35 555 b 50 000 – 29 999

c 71 000 – 43 001 d 80 003 – 39 999

Answer the calculations and show your working out. Explain why you chose the method you did.

Written subtraction (2)

- Subtract whole numbers with 5 and 6 digits using the formal written method
- Estimate and check the answer to a calculation

First estimate then calculate the answers to these calculations.

Example

53 262 - 27 051 → 53 300 – 27 100 = 26 200

```
  4  13
  5̸  3̸  2  6  2
– 2  7  0  5  1
  2  6  2  1  1
```

a 18 627 – 13 541 b 26 925 – 12 351 c 28 468 – 15 713

d 33 583 – 21 139 e 35 795 – 18 314 f 42 376 – 20 524

g 47 438 – 24 217 h 46 976 – 32 839 i 52 573 – 35 241

j 57 358 – 34 607 k 62 283 – 45 163 l 67 482 – 41 821

1 First estimate then calculate the answers to these calculations.

a 31 832 – 14 954 b 37 254 – 23 576 c 42 517 – 27 641

d 53 392 – 34 817 e 61 583 – 25 626 f 75 447 – 32 798

g 83 495 – 47 197 h 89 126 – 52 577 i 93 632 – 47 154

2 First estimate then calculate the answers to these calculations.

a 276 287 – 138 149 b 328 271 – 154 546 c 382 255 – 158 637

d 417 582 – 261 735 e 462 482 – 180 295 f 505 276 – 213 538

g 526 387 – 253 719 h 638 251 – 351 786 i 631 376 – 250 199

3 Use rounding to the nearest multiple of 100 to check your answers to Questions 1 and 2.

You will need:
- 0–9 dice
- ruler

4 Copy this 3 x 6 grid into your book and add a subtraction sign on the left hand side as shown.

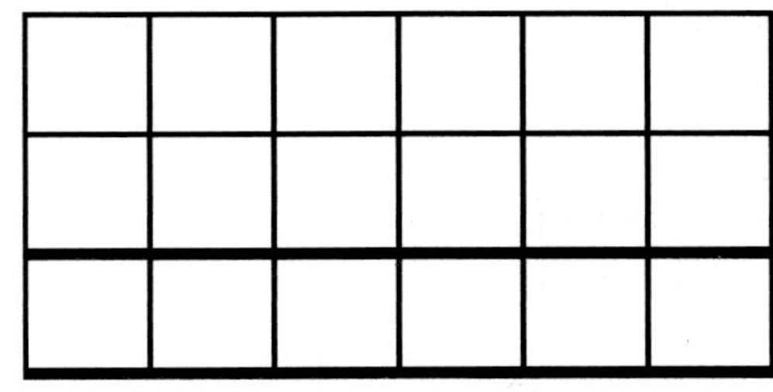

- Roll the dice twelve times. After each roll, write the digit you roll in one of the boxes in the top two rows of your grid. Make sure that the 6-digit number in the top row is larger than the 6-digit number in the second row.
- When the top two rows are complete, use the formal written method to answer the calculation.

hallenge 3

1 First estimate then calculate the answers to these calculations.

a 475 376 – 281 598 b 523 364 – 350 685 c 547 475 – 219 696

d 639 282 – 345 593 e 678 506 – 249 728 f 738 836 – 462 858

g 751 362 – 286 529 h 792 617 – 315 848 i 802 652 – 245 276

j 836 195 – 362 497 k 926 635 – 478 286 l 955 472 – 528 984

2 Use rounding to the nearest multiple of 100 to check your answers to Questions 1a to 1f.

3 What other methods could you use to check the answers to your calculations? Use your methods to check your answers to Questions 1g to 1l.

4 Write ten calculations for a partner to work out. Think of ways to make them challenging.

Adding and subtracting decimals

1 Work out these calculations using the formal written method.

a 376·86 + 215·11
b 235·31 + 453·47
c 415·74 + 143·63
d 283·54 + 304·83
e 327·68 + 250·61
f 311·75 + 185·92
g 436·33 + 281·94
h 193·81 + 542·57
i 352·72 + 483·45
j 462·72 + 311·53

Example

```
  3 5 4 · 8 3
+ 1 3 2 · 7 4
  4 8 7 · 5 7
      1
```

2 Work out these calculations using the formal written method.

a 372·65 – 130·41
b 457·87 – 245·63
c 376·26 – 143·50
d 566·47 – 213·72
e 763·57 – 340·83
f 699·45 – 247·61
g 857·04 – 461·28
h 714·56 – 353·84
i 826·38 – 561·72
j 682·53 – 291·62

Example

```
  5 14
  6̸ 4̸ 7 · 3 7
– 2 6 1 · 2 6
  3 8 6 · 1 1
```

3 What is the most challenging step when adding and subtracting decimals using the formal written method?

1 Work out these calculations using the formal written method.

a 2656·62 + 3712·57
b 3723·83 + 2195·42
c 4622·47 + 2183·71
d 1863·49 + 3715·80
e 3275·74 + 5341·53
f 6298·47 + 2540·82
g 3951·28 + 5356·81
h 5884·72 + 6417·45
i 7693·87 + 6403·74
j 8054·53 + 5321·71

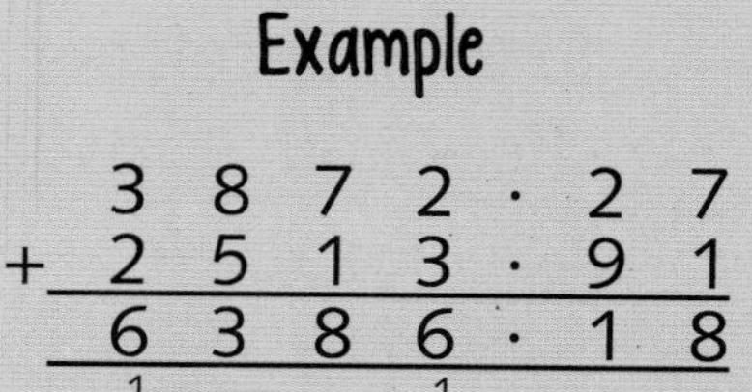

2 Work out these calculations using the formal written method.

a 6483·72 – 2150·91

b 5286·64 – 1074·83

c 5649·37 – 3823·75

d 4248·68 – 2016·98

e 6527·16 – 3274·54

f 7362·36 – 4851·44

g 8827·27 – 3656·36

h 9242·47 – 5570·61

i 9726·35 – 6851·77

j 8650·76 – 4723·49

Example

```
  6 13    1     17
  7  3 9  2 ·  7 5
– 2  6 3  1 ·  9 3
  4  7 6  0 ·  8 2
```

3 Think of a time when you might need to add or subtract decimals using the written method.

Challenge 3

1 Work out these calculations using the formal written method.

a 12 416·54 + 25 276·81

b 25 376·38 + 37 152·90

c 28 376·16 + 31 573·85

d 36 282·48 + 37 355·62

e 48 275·37 + 21 953·71

f 56 486·62 + 37 365·57

g 43 826·75 + 52 738·43

h 63 583·47 + 58 375·92

i 78 362·92 + 64 365·67

j 47 836·73 + 75 649·58

2 Work out these calculations using the formal written method.

a 37 872·36 – 13 694·51

b 42 376·28 – 15 381·36

c 48 286·27 – 23 537·48

d 52 737·62 – 34 381·72

e 67 427·62 – 42 816·98

f 78 329·82 – 54 163·29

g 88 331·13 – 62 770·42

h 81 932·62 – 73 855·28

i 55 555·55 – 27 777·77

j 82 486·26 – 37 294·55

Naming angles

Name and measure acute, obtuse and reflex angles

You will need:

- protractor

Rule

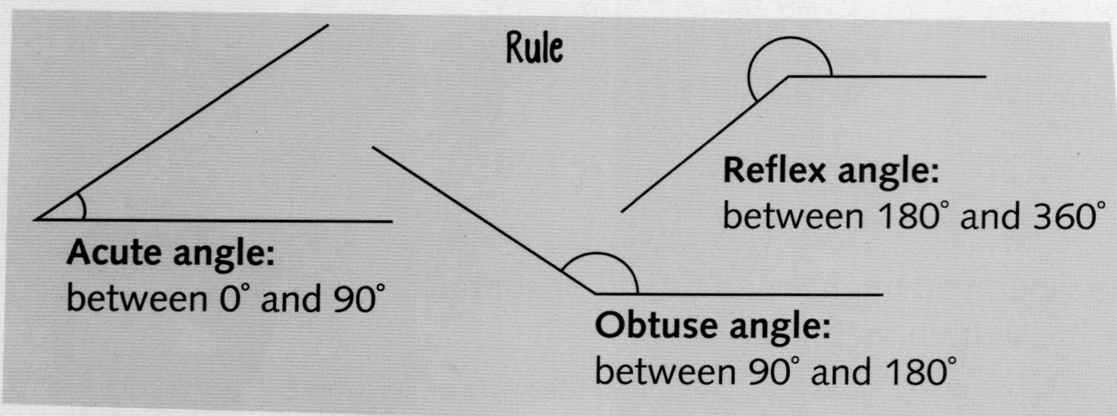

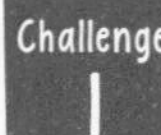

1 Use your protractor to help you decide whether the angle of each pizza slice is acute, obtuse or reflex.
Name each angle.

Example

x

angle **x**: acute

2 Write the angles of the pizza slices in order, beginning with the smallest angle.

Challenge 2

1 Use your protractor to help you decide whether each angle is acute, obtuse or reflex. Name each angle.

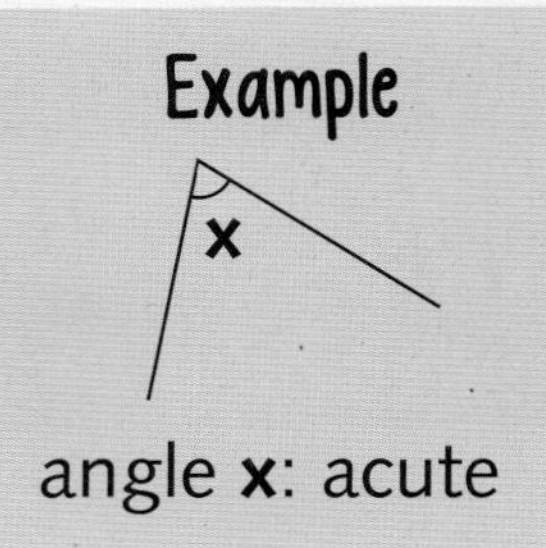

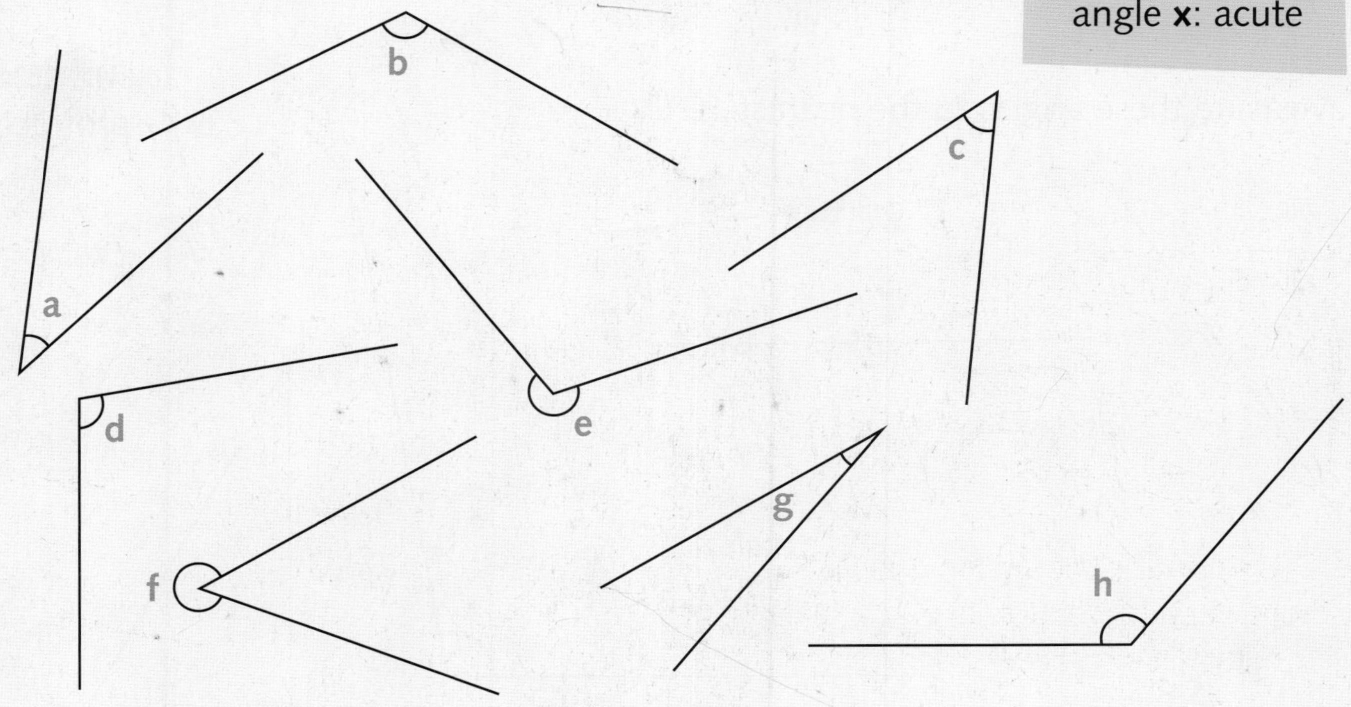

2 Write the letters of the angles that are:

a less than one right angle

b greater than two right angles

c less than two right angles and greater than one right angle

3 Write the letter of the angle that is greater than three right angles.

Challenge 3

Draw one or more diagrams to answer each question.

a Is it possible to fit together two acute angles to make an obtuse angle?

b Is it possible to fit together two obtuse angles to make a reflex angle?

c Is it possible to fit together three acute angles to make a reflex angle?

Measuring angles

Measure and draw angles to the nearest 5°

Measure these angles to the nearest 10°.

You will need:
- protractor

Example

x

x = 60°

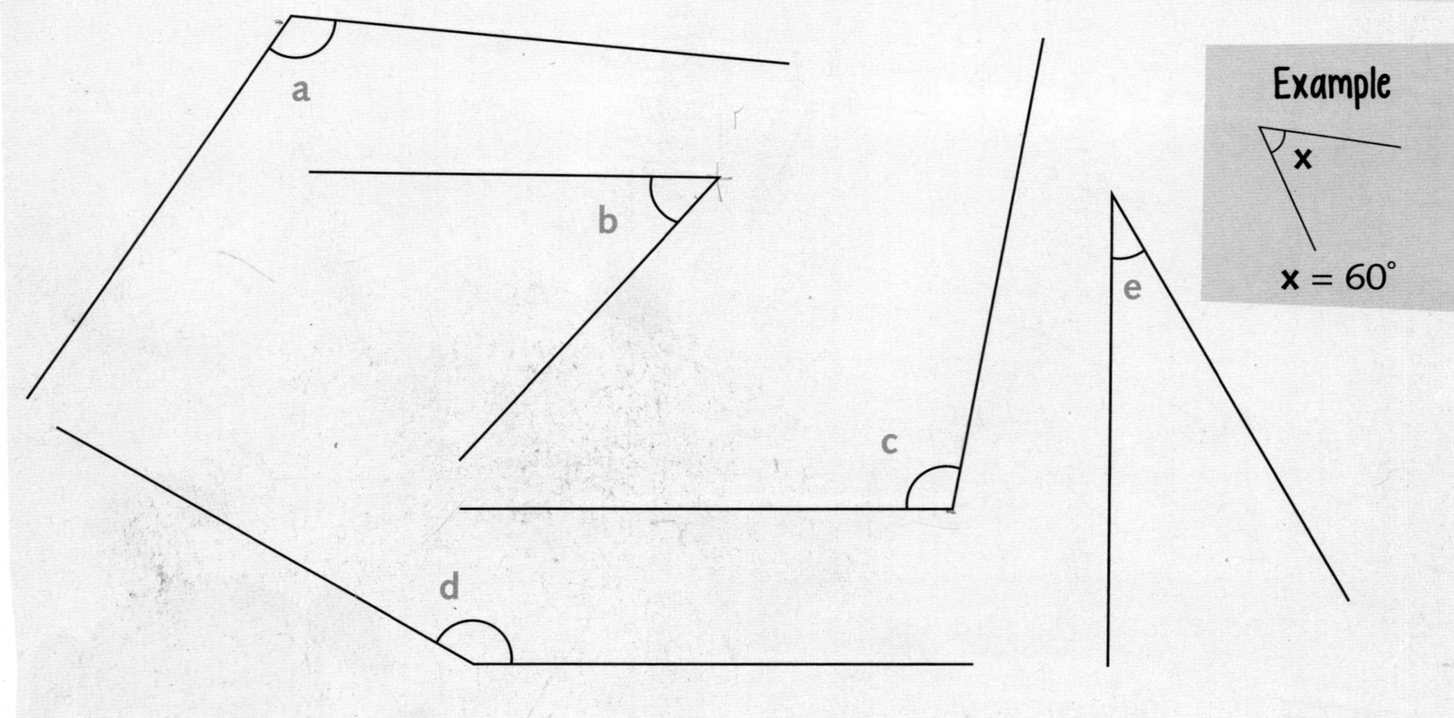

Challenge 2

1 Measure these angles to the nearest 5°.

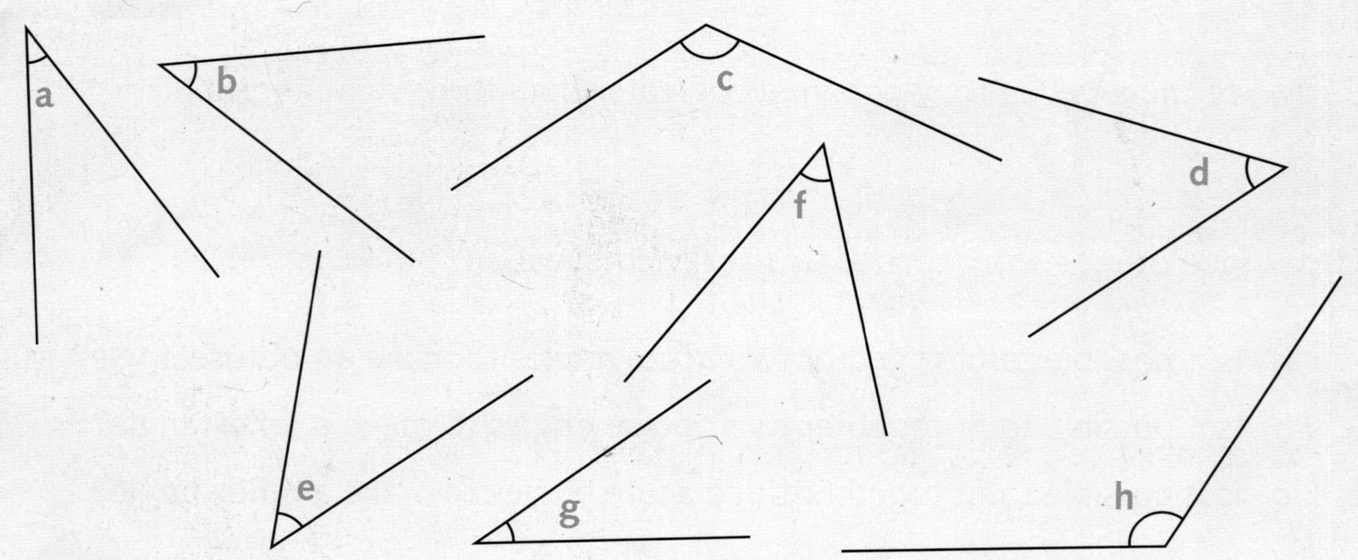

2 List the pairs of angles in Question 1 that are the same size.

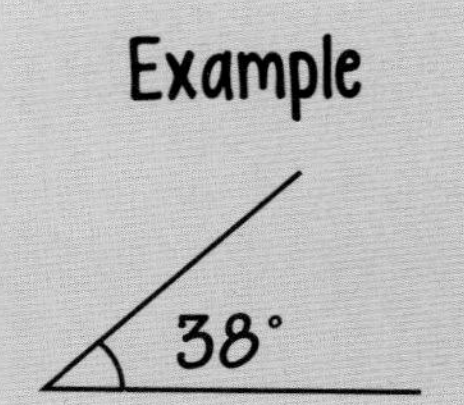

3 Draw and label these acute angles.

a 40° b 60° c 25°

d 75° e 50° f 45°

4 Draw and label these obtuse angles.

a 110° b 150° c 95°

d 125° e 165° f 140°

Challenge 3

1 Measure the marked angles in these 2-D shapes. Write your answers in degrees.

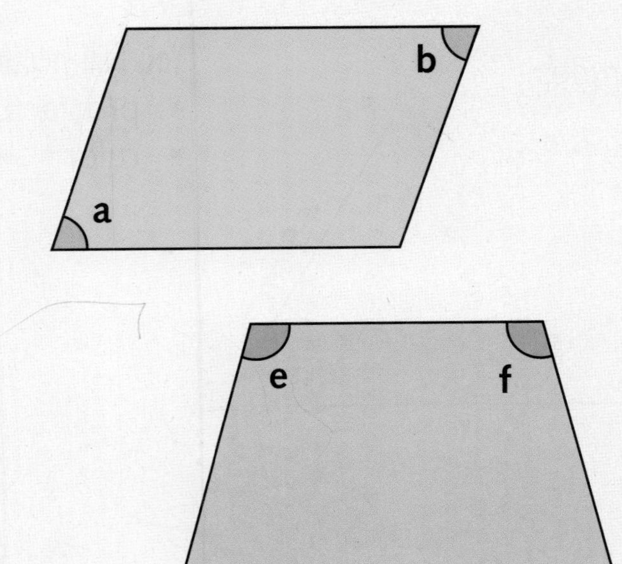

2 Write what you notice about your answers.

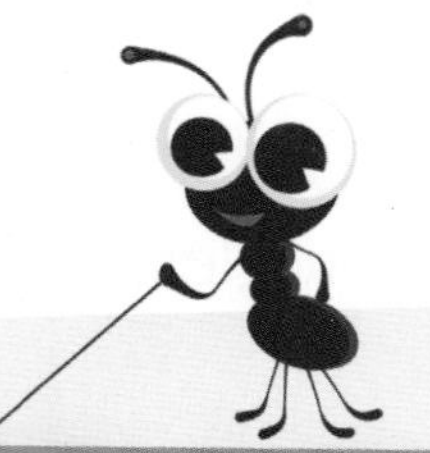

Drawing angles

Use a ruler and protractor to make accurate drawings of angles

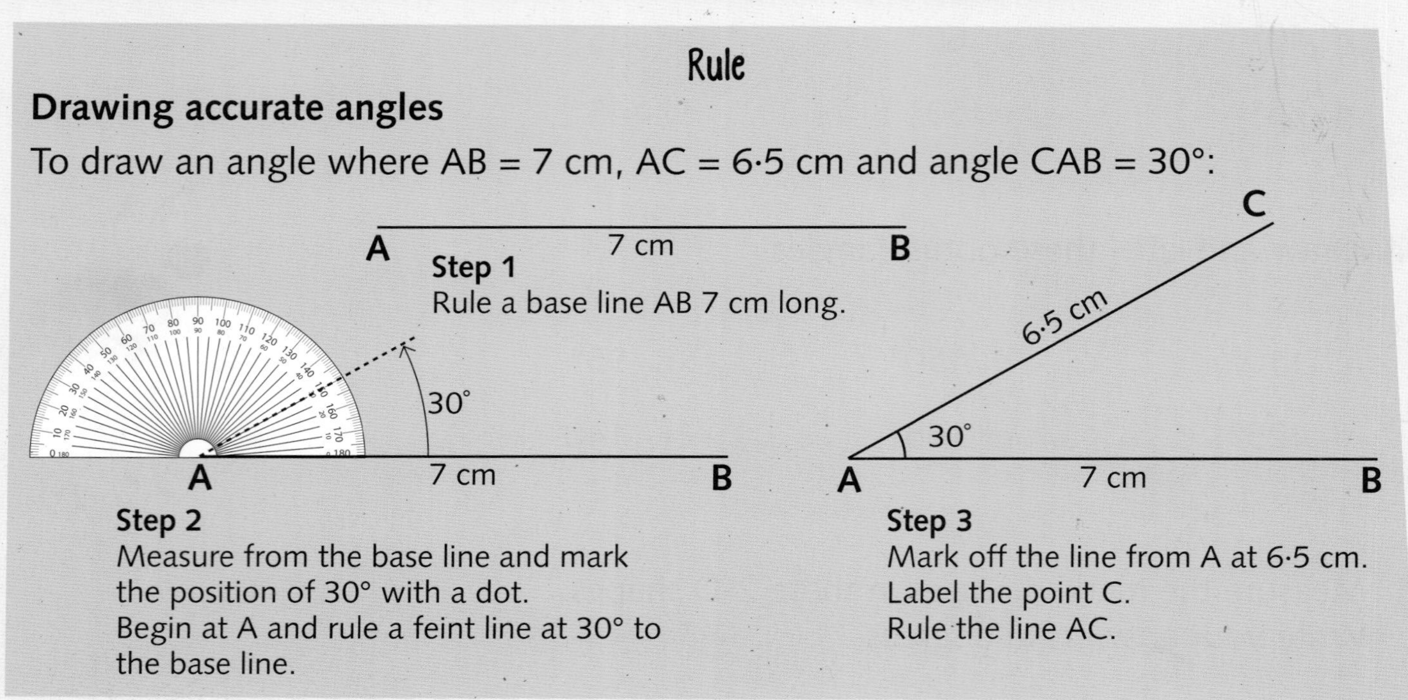

Rule

Drawing accurate angles

To draw an angle where AB = 7 cm, AC = 6·5 cm and angle CAB = 30°:

A
7 cm
B

Step 1
Rule a base line AB 7 cm long.

30°
A
7 cm
B

Step 2
Measure from the base line and mark the position of 30° with a dot.
Begin at A and rule a feint line at 30° to the base line.

C
6·5 cm
30°
A
7 cm
B

Step 3
Mark off the line from A at 6·5 cm.
Label the point C.
Rule the line AC.

Challenge 1

You will need:
- protractor
- ruler

1 Make accurate drawings of these acute angles.

a

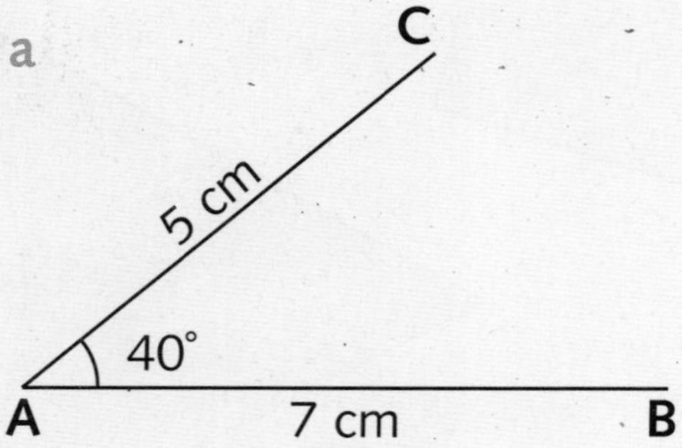

C
5 cm
40°
A
7 cm
B

b

F
4·5 cm
60°
D
7 cm
E

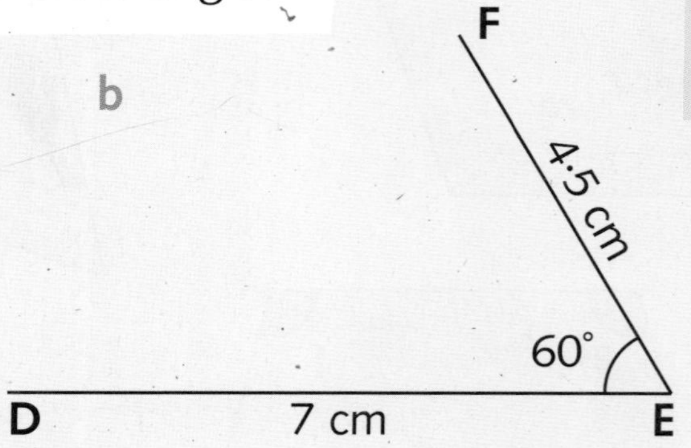

2 Make accurate drawings of these obtuse angles.

a

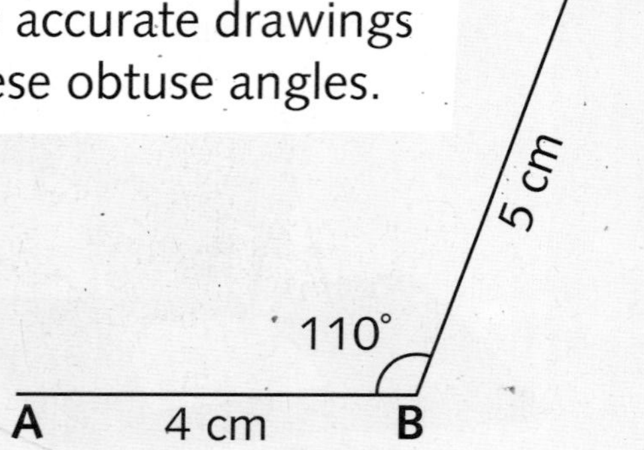

C
5 cm
110°
A
4 cm
B

b

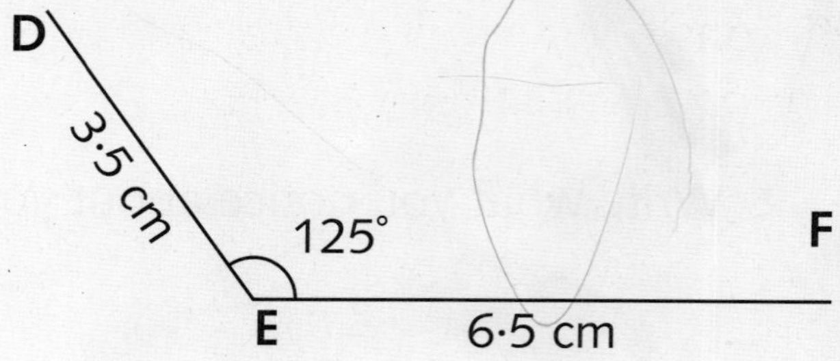

D
3·5 cm
125°
E
6·5 cm
F

Challenge 2

1 Make accurate drawings of these angles.

a

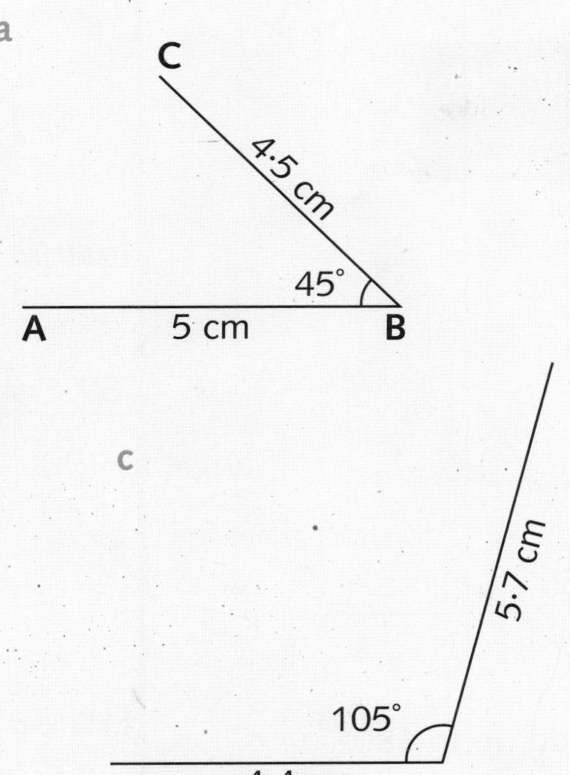

b

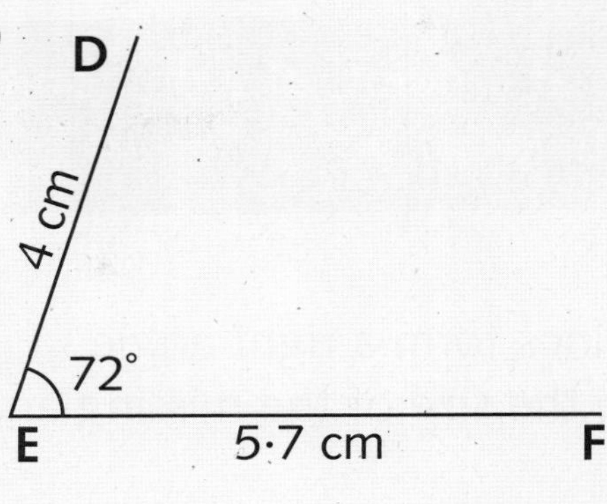

c

d 5·5 cm

126°

6·2 cm

2 Make accurate drawings of these angles.

a
- AB = 7 cm
- BC = 4·5 cm
- angle ABC = 55°

b
- DE = 6·3 cm
- EF = 8·2 cm
- angle DEF = 123°

3 Use your ruler and protractor to construct a square that has sides of 6 cm.

Challenge 3

Construct a regular hexagon that has sides of 6·5 cm and angles of 120°.

Identifying angles

Identify angles at a point, at a point on a straight line and other multiples of 90°

Challenge 1

1 The red lines form a right angle.
Calculate the size of the missing angle.

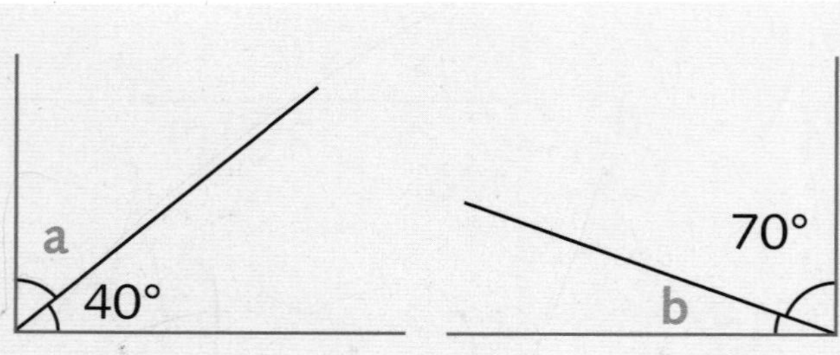

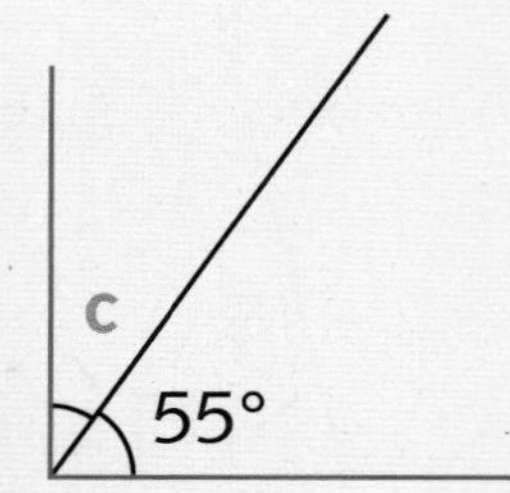

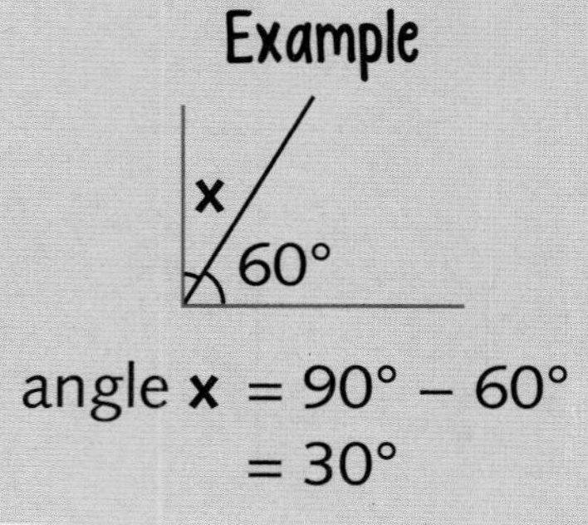

2 The red line is a straight line. The angles add up to 180°.
Calculate the size of the missing angle.

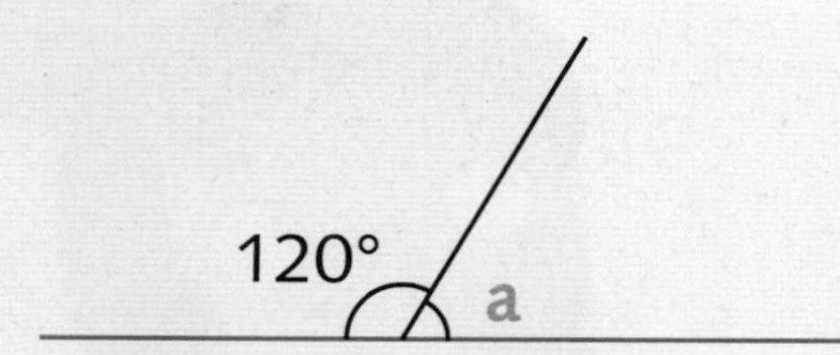

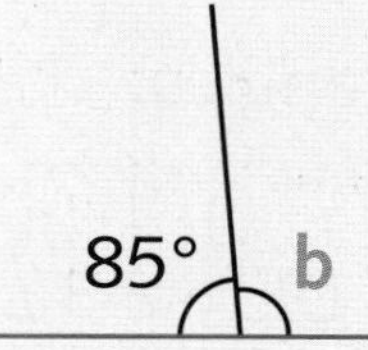

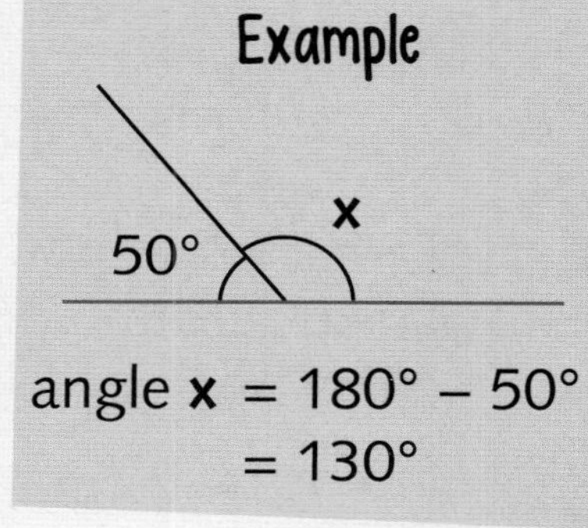

Challenge 2

1 These angles are at a point on a straight line and make a half turn.
Calculate the size of each unknown angle.

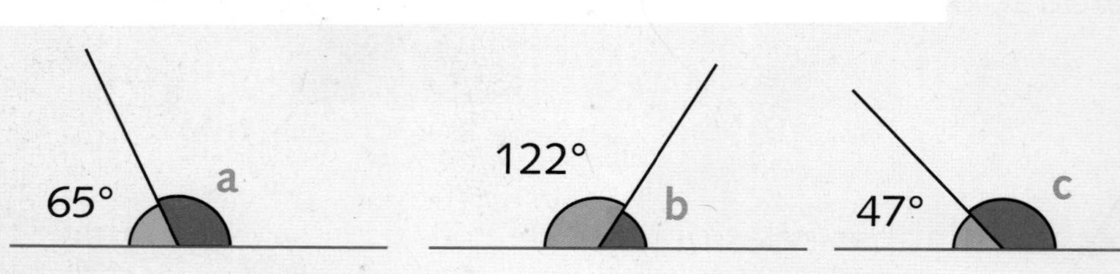

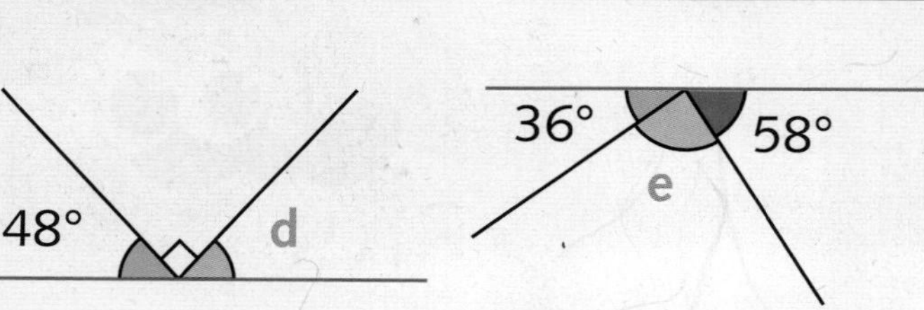

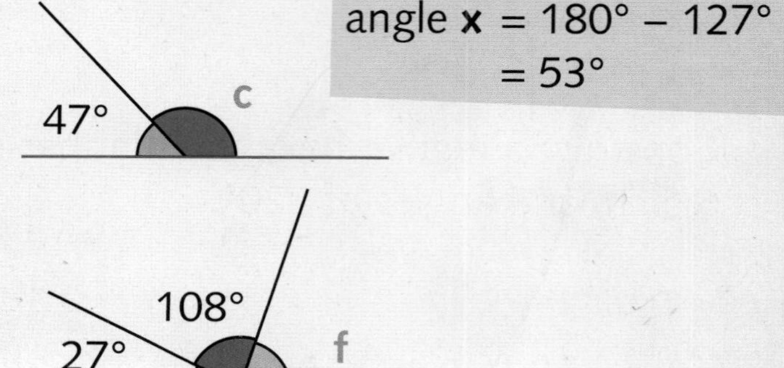

2 These angles are at a point and make one whole turn. Name and calculate the size of the shaded angles.

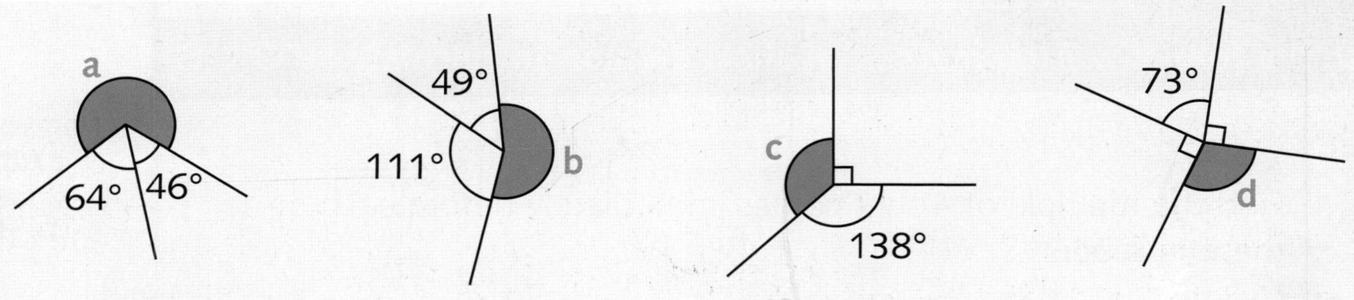

3 Calculate the size of each unknown angle.

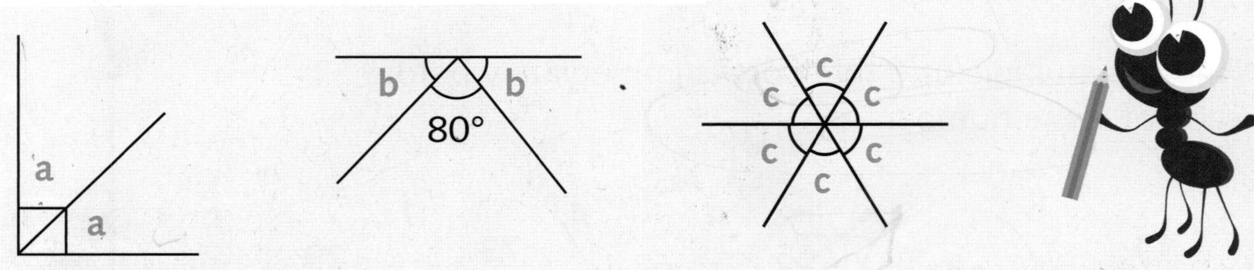

Challenge 3

Measure the yellow and green angles.
Calculate the orange angle then measure to check.
Find the total of the three angles in each diagram.

You will need:
- protractor

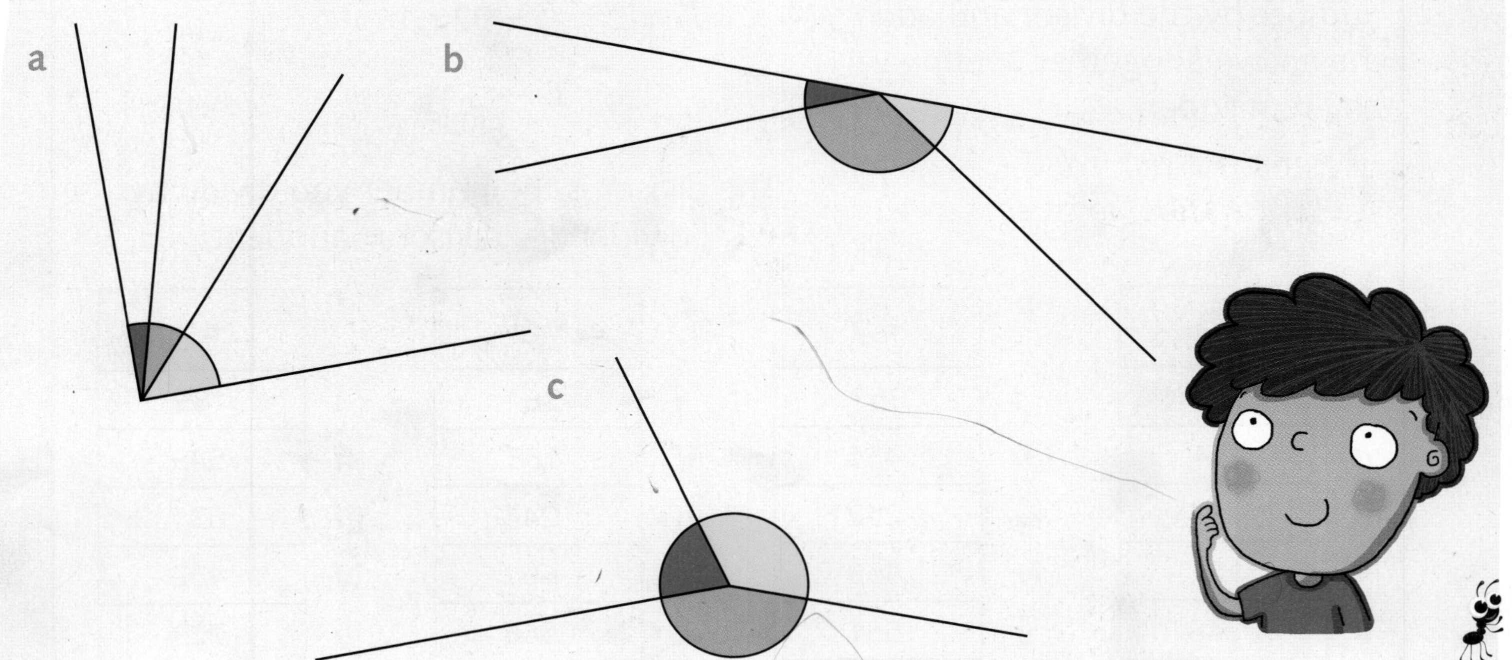

Division HTO ÷ O with a remainder

Use the formal written method of short division to calculate HTO ÷ O

Challenge 1

Example

15 → 12

1 Find the multiple of 4 that comes immediately before each of these numbers.

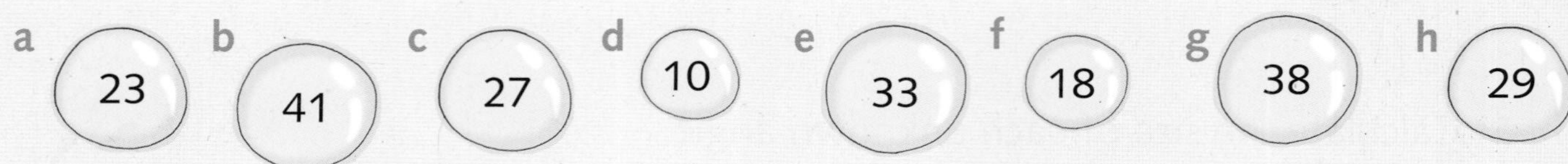

a 23 b 41 c 27 d 10 e 33 f 18 g 38 h 29

2 Find the multiple of 6 that comes immediately before each of these numbers.

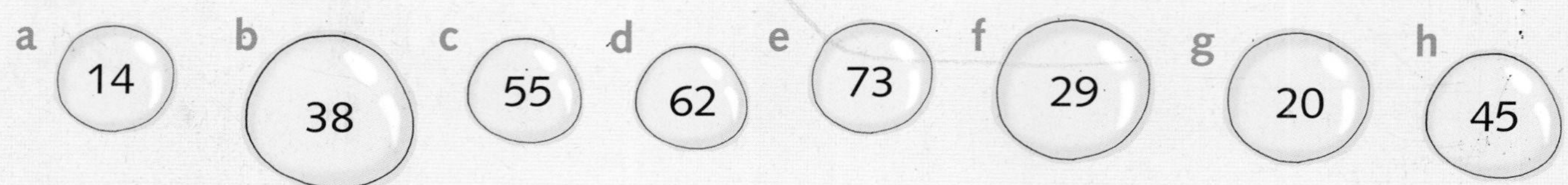

a 14 b 38 c 55 d 62 e 73 f 29 g 20 h 45

3 Partition each 3-digit number into a multiple of 10 and a 1-digit number. Divide each number by the divisor and add the answers together, writing any remainder.

Example

277 ÷ 3 = (270 + 7) ÷ 3
= 90 + 2 r 1
= 92 r 1

Rule

The divisor is the number you divide by.
dividend ÷ divisor = quotient

	a ÷ 3	b ÷ 5	c ÷ 6	d ÷ 9
i	219	357	367	189
ii	154	455	188	549
iii	334	252	246	631
iv	157	458	661	452
v	248	551	546	723

Challenge 2

1 For each division calculation estimate the answer, then use the formal written method to work out the answer. Remember to record any remainders.

Example

279 ÷ 6 → 300 ÷ 6 = 50

```
   H T O
     4 6 r3
6 | 2 7 ³9
```

a 465 ÷ 5	b 258 ÷ 4	c 372 ÷ 9	d 285 ÷ 4
e 495 ÷ 4	f 666 ÷ 8	g 387 ÷ 6	h 264 ÷ 3
i 198 ÷ 5	j 556 ÷ 9	k 375 ÷ 7	l 870 ÷ 9

2 Write two calculations for each instruction.

a Divide a 3-digit number by 9 to give an answer that is an odd number.

b Divide a 3-digit number by 6 to give an answer that is even.

c Divide a 3-digit number by 8 to give one answer with an odd number and one answer with an even number.

Can you find the calculations that have a remainder without doing any written working out? For each calculation write either the remainder or 'no remainder'. Explain how you know.

a 326 ÷ 5	b 488 ÷ 4	c 463 ÷ 5	d 284 ÷ 4
e 165 ÷ 4	f 646 ÷ 8	g 387 ÷ 6	h 815 ÷ 9
i 198 ÷ 2	j 333 ÷ 4	k 357 ÷ 7	l 841 ÷ 2
m 6473 ÷ 5	n 7260 ÷ 9	o 4632 ÷ 20	p 3760 ÷ 10

Division HTO ÷ O with a fraction remainder

Use the formal written method of short division to calculate HTO ÷ O with a fraction remainder

The multiples below are all jumbled.
Sort them into multiples of 6, 7, 8 and 9. You may use the same multiple more than once.

Example

Multiples of 6: 24, 36, ...

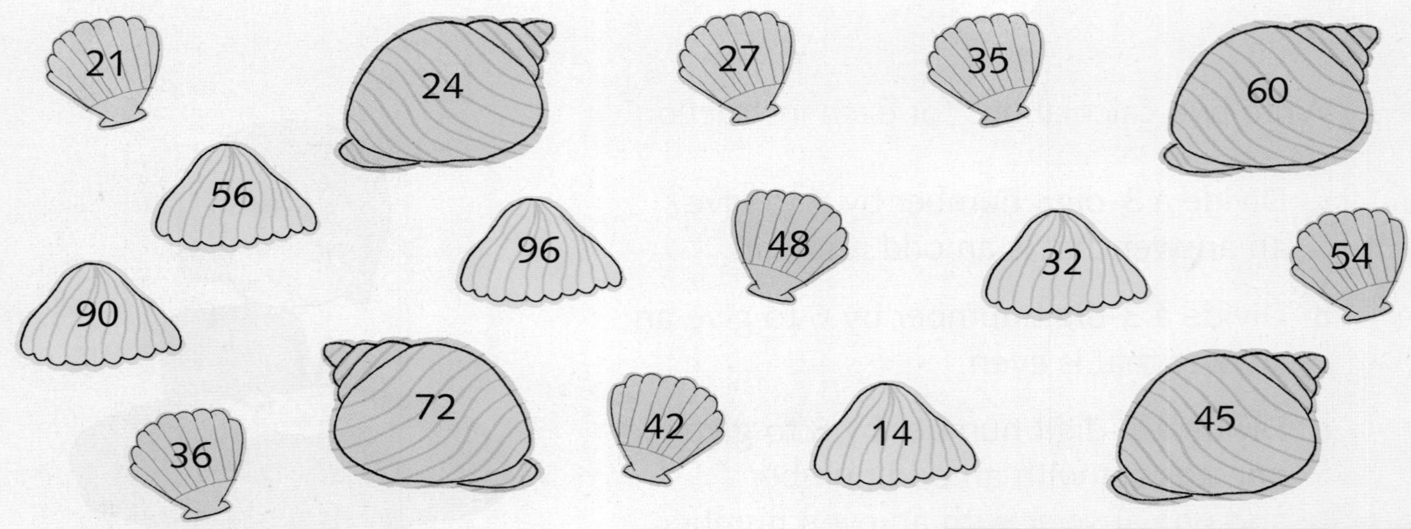

1 For each division calculation write your estimate, then use the formal written method to work out the answer. Record any remainders as a fraction.

Example

276 ÷ 8 → 240 ÷ 8 = 30

```
    H  T  O
       3  4 r 4 = 34 4/8 = 34 1/2
8 | 2  7  ³6
```

a 345 ÷ 4	b 458 ÷ 8	c 672 ÷ 9
d 186 ÷ 4	e 491 ÷ 4	f 266 ÷ 8
g 375 ÷ 6	h 284 ÷ 3	i 198 ÷ 5
j 566 ÷ 6	k 275 ÷ 3	l 873 ÷ 9

2 Write two calculations for each instruction.

a Divide a 3-digit number by 5 to give a remainder of 3.

b Divide a 3-digit number by 4 to give a remainder of 2.

c Divide a 3-digit number by 7 to give a remainder of 6.

Challenge 3

Write a calculation to match each of the clues.

a When I divide a 3-digit number by 4 my answer has a remainder of $\frac{1}{4}$.

b When I divide a 2-digit number by 6 my answer has a remainder of $\frac{1}{2}$.

c When I divide a 3-digit number by 5 my answer has a remainder of $\frac{3}{5}$.

d When I divide a 3-digit number greater than 300 but less than 360 by 4 my answer has a remainder of $\frac{3}{4}$.

e When I divide a 3-digit odd number between 500 and 700 by 8 my answer has a remainder of $\frac{1}{4}$.

f When I divide a 2-digit number by 8 my answer has a remainder of $\frac{1}{4}$.

g When I divide a 3-digit number greater than 900 by 6 my answer has a remainder of $\frac{1}{3}$.

h When I divide a 3-digit number by 4 my answer has a fractional remainder that can be simplified.

i When I divide the same 3-digit number by 2 different divisors my answer has a remainder of $\frac{1}{3}$.

Division HTO ÷ O with a decimal remainder

Use the formal written method of short division to calculate HTO ÷ O with a decimal remainder

Challenge 1

1 Find the multiple of 3 that comes immediately before each of these numbers.

Example

14 → 12

2 Find the multiple of 8 that comes immediately before each of these numbers.

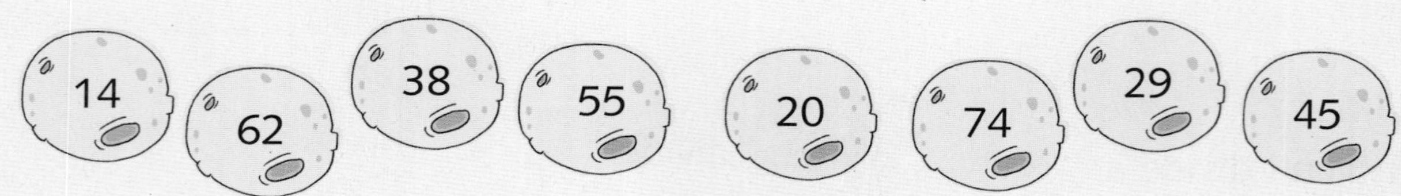

3 Write these whole numbers as tenths.

Example

7 = 70 tenths

4 Write these tenths as hundredths.

Example

0·9 = 90 hundredths

0·2 0·1 0·4 0·6 0·3 0·5 0·9 0·7

Challenge 2

For each division calculation estimate the answer, then use the formal written method to work out the answer. Record any remainders as a decimal.

Example

$376 \div 5 \rightarrow 400 \div 5 = 80$

```
    H  T  O
       7  5 · 2
5 | 3  7 ²6 ·¹0
```

a $164 \div 5$ b $198 \div 4$ c $375 \div 6$

d $186 \div 4$ e $491 \div 5$ f $275 \div 4$

g $632 \div 8$ h $245 \div 6$ i $438 \div 4$

j $526 \div 6$ k $396 \div 8$ l $773 \div 5$

1 Find the answers to these problems.

a A group of 5 friends won a competition. They equally shared the £852 prize money. How much did each person win?

b A train took 5 hours to complete a journey of 673 km. If the train travelled the same distance each hour, how many kilometres did it travel in 1 hour?

c Belal's phone bill was £453 for 6 months. What is the cost on average per month?

d Samina spent £348 on 8 pairs of shoes. How much did she spend on average per pair of shoes?

e Ronan spent $\frac{1}{3}$ of the amount that Chris spent on computer games. If Chris spent £537, how much did Ronan spend?

2 Make up a word problem similar to those in Question 1 that has an answer of £27.25.

3 Explain how 43 r 2, 43·25 and $43\frac{1}{4}$ can all be the same answer to a division calculation.

4 Can you think of five situations when you are most likely to require an answer with a decimal remainder?

Solving word problems: rounding remainders

Solve division problems including answers that involve rounding remainders up or down

Challenge 1

Write the answers to these division calculations. Remember to record any remainders.

a 76 ÷ 9	b 48 ÷ 5	c 67 ÷ 8	d 58 ÷ 6
e 86 ÷ 8	f 59 ÷ 9	g 67 ÷ 7	h 76 ÷ 9
i 37 ÷ 4	j 88 ÷ 9	k 52 ÷ 6	l 39 ÷ 7

Challenge 2

Find the answer to each of the word problems. If there is a remainder think carefully about whether it needs to be rounded up or down to fit the question.

a The sandwich stall made 382 sandwiches. They were packed into boxes, each containing 6 sandwiches. How many full boxes could be made?

b In one day 587 people went on the ghost train. The train holds 8 people. How many times did the train need to run?

c Candy floss costs £3 per bag. A total of 265 bags were sold in one day. How much money was taken?

d The rollercoaster seats 9 people. A total of 123 people are waiting in the queue. How many times does the rollercoaster need to run before everyone in the queue has had a ride?

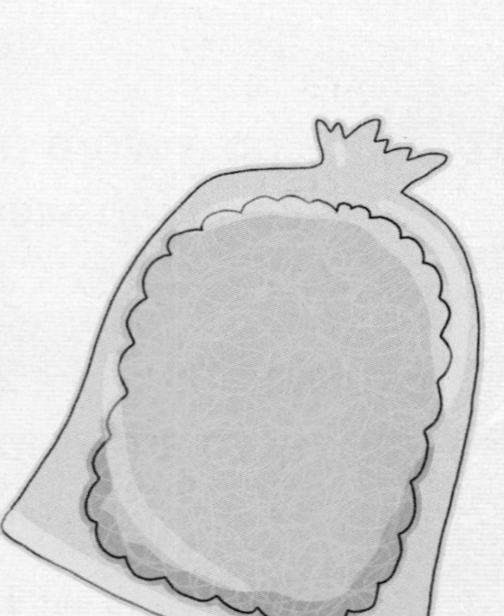

e The Smythe family has £472 to spend on rides. All rides cost £5. How many ride tickets can they buy?

f Doughnuts are sold in packs of 4. There are 673 doughnuts to be packaged. How many packs can be made?

g At the end of the day the hot dog stall counted £543 in the till. Hot dogs cost £4 each. How many had they sold?

h Each dodgem car holds 2 people. In one day 435 people rode in the dodgem cars. How many dodgem car rides were made?

i A family of 2 adults and 4 children go to the fairground. Entrance to the fairground costs £43 for adults and £26 for children. The family has allowed £180 for entrance fees. Do they have enough money?

Write your own word problems that involve rounding up or down for each of these calculations. The arrow ↑ means to round the answer up. The arrow ↓ means to round the answer down. Swap them with a partner to solve.

a $263 \div 4$ ↑ b $468 \div 5$ ↓

c $669 \div 8$ ↓ d $321 \div 6$ ↑

e $300 \div 7$ ↑ f $558 \div 7$ ↑

g $729 \div 6$ ↓ h $198 \div 4$ ↓

Thousandths

Recognise and use thousandths and relate them to tenths and hundredths

What fraction of each diagram is shaded blue?

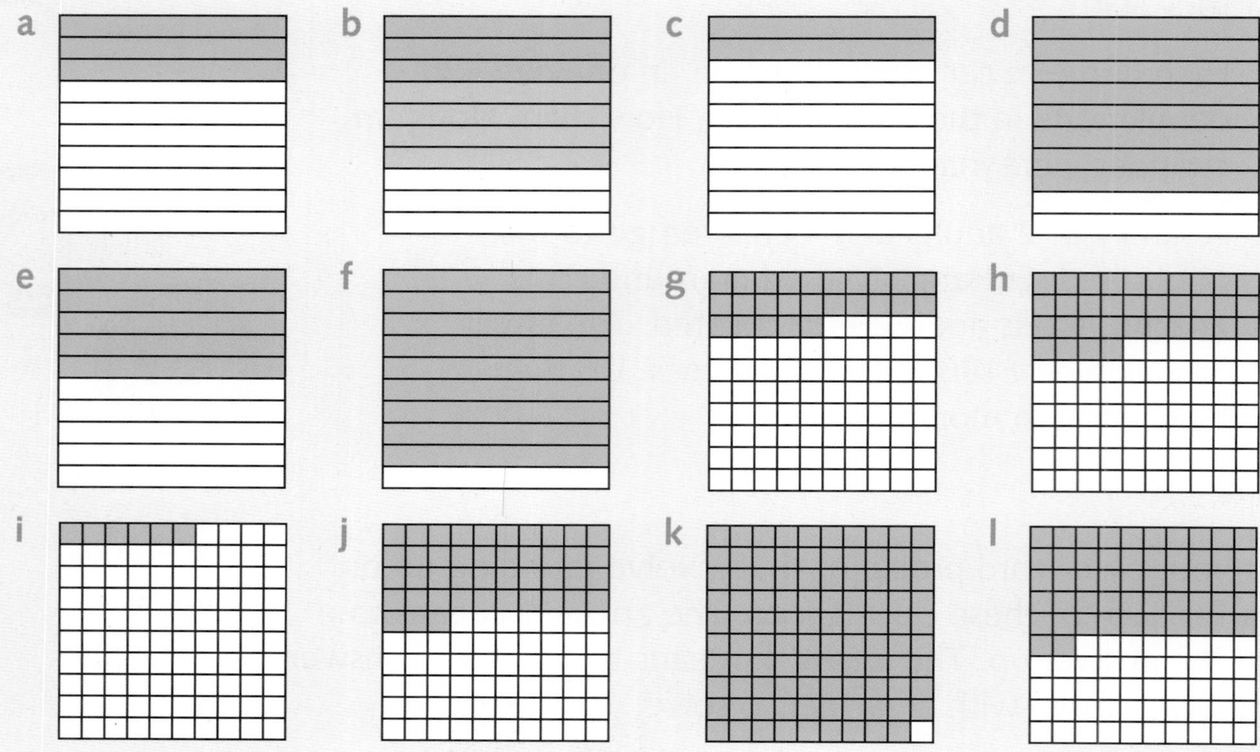

1 How many thousandths are shaded? Write your answer as a fraction.

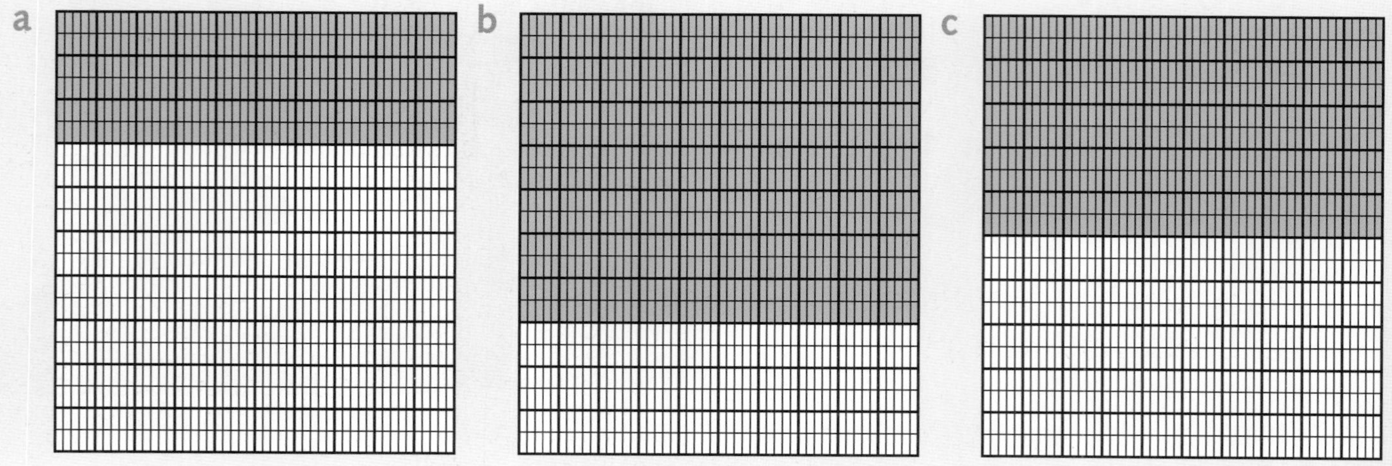

d 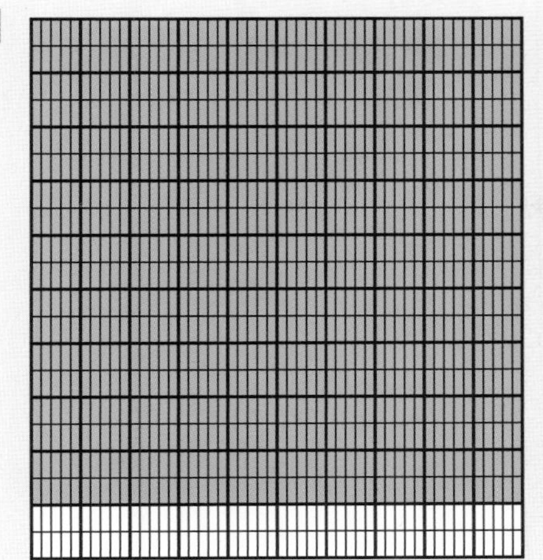

e 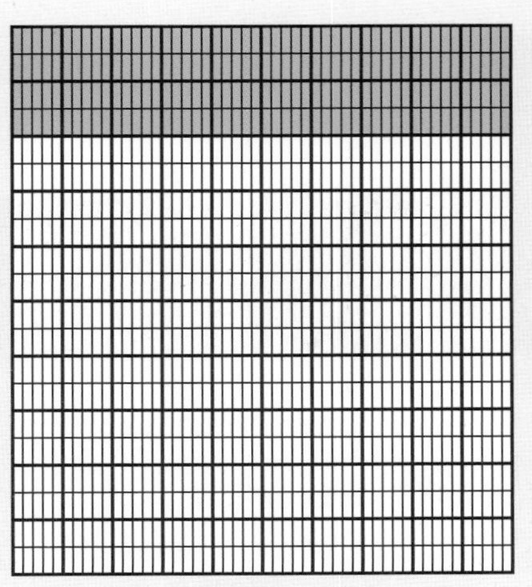

f 

2 Which of the diagrams in Question 1 is equivalent to a half? How do you know?

3 Look at the diagrams in Question 1 and write the equivalent tenths and hundredths.

Challenge 3

1 Complete these equivalent fractions.

a $\frac{1}{10} = \frac{}{100} = \frac{}{1000}$ b $\frac{7}{10} = \frac{}{100} = \frac{}{1000}$ c $\frac{4}{10} = \frac{}{100} = \frac{}{1000}$

d $\frac{9}{10} = \frac{}{100} = \frac{}{1000}$ e $\frac{2}{10} = \frac{}{100} = \frac{}{1000}$ f $\frac{5}{10} = \frac{}{100} = \frac{}{1000}$

2 Complete these equivalent fractions.

a $\frac{23}{100} = \frac{}{1000}$ b $\frac{65}{100} = \frac{}{1000}$ c $\frac{48}{100} = \frac{}{1000}$

d $\frac{81}{100} = \frac{}{1000}$ e $\frac{14}{100} = \frac{}{1000}$ f $\frac{75}{100} = \frac{}{1000}$

g What is $\frac{75}{100}$ also equivalent to?

3 Why are the fractions of tenths, hundredths and thousandths related?

Fractions in order

Compare and order fractions whose denominators are all multiples of the same number

Challenge 1

Order these pairs of fractions, smallest to largest.

- Write out the multiples of the denominators to find the lowest common multiple (LCM).
- Change each fraction to its equivalent.
- Order the fractions.

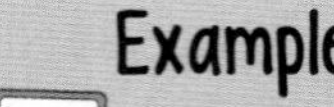

Example

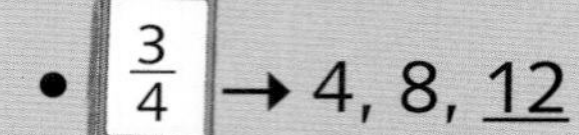

- $\frac{3}{4}$ → 4, 8, <u>12</u>

  $\frac{1}{3}$ → 3, 6, 9, <u>12</u>

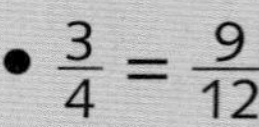

- $\frac{3}{4} = \frac{9}{12}$

  $\frac{1}{3} = \frac{4}{12}$

- $\frac{1}{3}, \frac{3}{4}$

12 is the lowest multiple they have in common so I am going to change all the fractions to twelfths.

a $\frac{9}{12}$ $\frac{1}{2}$ b $\frac{2}{5}$ $\frac{3}{4}$ c $\frac{7}{9}$ $\frac{2}{3}$ d $\frac{11}{15}$ $\frac{1}{5}$

e $\frac{5}{8}$ $\frac{3}{4}$ f $\frac{2}{7}$ $\frac{1}{3}$ g $\frac{5}{6}$ $\frac{2}{3}$ h $\frac{16}{20}$ $\frac{3}{5}$

Challenge 2

1 Order these sets of fractions, smallest to largest.

a $\frac{9}{12}$ $\frac{1}{2}$ $\frac{1}{3}$ b $\frac{2}{5}$ $\frac{3}{4}$ $\frac{1}{2}$ c $\frac{7}{9}$ $\frac{2}{3}$ $\frac{14}{18}$

d $\frac{11}{15}$ $\frac{1}{5}$ $\frac{2}{3}$ e $\frac{5}{8}$ $\frac{3}{4}$ $\frac{10}{16}$ f $\frac{2}{7}$ $\frac{1}{3}$ $\frac{5}{21}$

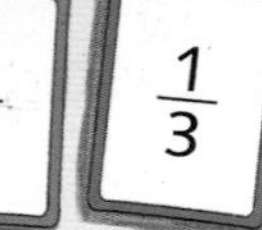

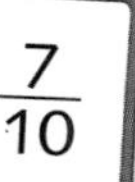

g $\frac{5}{6}$ $\frac{2}{3}$ $\frac{1}{3}$ h $\frac{16}{20}$ $\frac{3}{5}$ $\frac{7}{10}$ i $\frac{3}{5}$ $\frac{7}{10}$ $\frac{1}{2}$

2 Would you rather have $\frac{8}{9}$ or $\frac{5}{6}$ of a chocolate bar? Draw a diagram of a chocolate bar to show the difference between the two fractions.

3 Would you rather work out $\frac{4}{7}$ or $\frac{3}{4}$ of a page of calculations? Explain your reason.

4 Write a 'Would you rather...?' question like those given in Questions 2 and 3 for your partner.

Challenge 3

1 Order these fractions, smallest to largest.

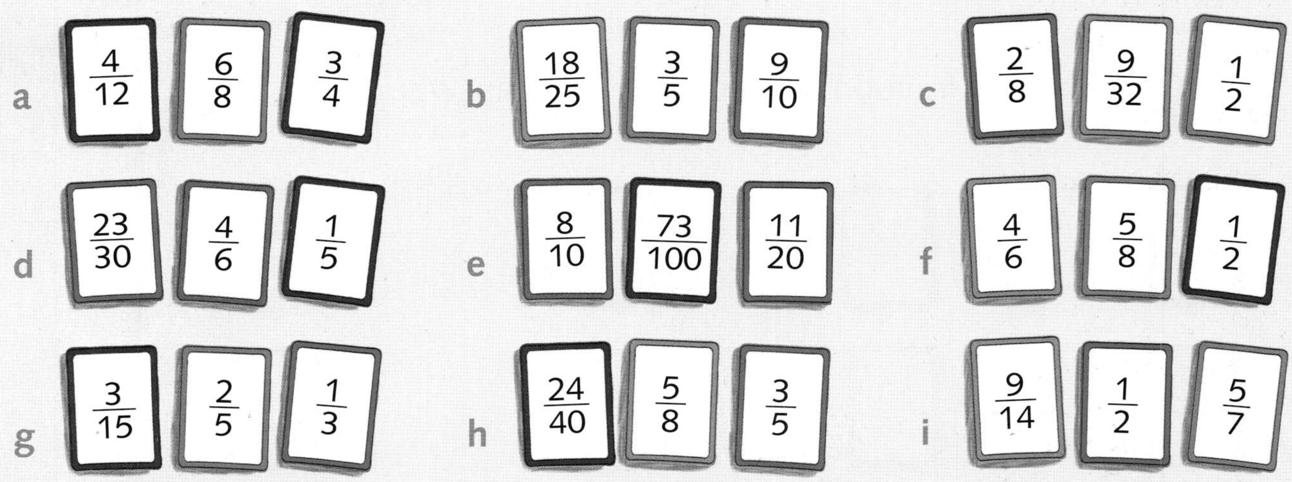

2 Use division to find two fractions that are equal to these fractions. What can the denominator and the numerator be divided by?

a $\frac{8}{24}$ b $\frac{12}{20}$ c $\frac{8}{12}$ d $\frac{24}{32}$

3 Explain how you worked out the answers in Question 2.

4 Use multiplication to find two fractions that are equal to these fractions.

a $\frac{4}{9}$ b $\frac{3}{7}$ c $\frac{6}{8}$ d $\frac{9}{11}$

Hint
Multiply the denominator and the numerator by the same number.

Adding fractions

Add fractions with the same denominator and denominators that are multiples of the same number

Challenge 1

1 Add these fractions.

a $\frac{3}{5} + \frac{1}{5}$ b $\frac{5}{8} + \frac{2}{8}$ c $\frac{4}{6} + \frac{3}{6}$ d $\frac{6}{8} + \frac{5}{8}$

e $\frac{4}{5} + \frac{3}{5}$ f $\frac{7}{10} + \frac{6}{10}$ g $\frac{6}{9} + \frac{8}{9}$ h $\frac{7}{12} + \frac{6}{12}$

2 Write two different fraction additions for each answer.

Example

$\frac{8}{11} = \frac{2}{11} + \frac{6}{11}$

$= \frac{5}{11} + \frac{3}{11}$

a  $\frac{7}{9}$ b 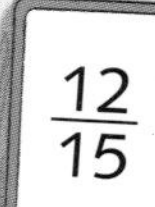 $\frac{12}{15}$ c  $\frac{7}{10}$ d $\frac{9}{11}$

e  $\frac{10}{12}$ f $\frac{13}{16}$ g $\frac{8}{13}$ h $\frac{14}{16}$

Challenge 2

1 Add these fractions.

a $\frac{2}{5} + \frac{6}{10}$ b $\frac{1}{2} + \frac{4}{10}$ c $\frac{2}{4} + \frac{1}{3}$ d $\frac{5}{10} + \frac{1}{2}$ e $\frac{1}{2} + \frac{1}{5}$

f $\frac{2}{3} + \frac{1}{2}$ g $\frac{5}{10} + \frac{1}{3}$ h $\frac{2}{3} + \frac{3}{4}$ i $\frac{1}{5} + \frac{3}{10}$ j $\frac{1}{3} + \frac{6}{5}$

k $\frac{1}{4} + \frac{3}{8}$ l $\frac{2}{5} + \frac{4}{10}$ m $\frac{3}{4} + \frac{1}{2}$ n $\frac{1}{6} + \frac{4}{12}$ o $\frac{2}{3} + \frac{4}{6}$

2 Look at Question 1d. This calculation could be done without converting the fraction. Explain how.

3 Work out these fraction problems.

a Louis and Amy are putting books away in the library. After ten minutes Louis has managed to put $\frac{1}{4}$ of the books away and Amy has put away $\frac{2}{3}$. What fraction of the books have they put away altogether?

b Sam is reading a really good book. Last night he read $\frac{1}{2}$ of it, and this morning he read another $\frac{3}{8}$. How much has he read so far?

c Annie got given some money for her birthday. She bought a new dress that used $\frac{3}{5}$ of her money and then she spent $\frac{1}{4}$ of her money on a matching bag. What fraction of her money is left?

d Jamila's mum is saving up for their holiday. One month she saved $\frac{3}{10}$ of the target amount; the next month she saved $\frac{2}{20}$ of the target. What fraction has she saved so far?

4 Write two fraction problems for a partner to work out.

Challenge 3

1 Add these fractions.

a	$\frac{6}{7} + \frac{1}{4}$	b	$\frac{3}{5} + \frac{13}{15}$	c	$\frac{2}{4} + \frac{1}{10}$	d	$\frac{4}{6} + \frac{1}{4}$	e	$\frac{3}{9} + \frac{2}{4}$
f	$\frac{2}{3} + \frac{3}{8}$	g	$\frac{4}{6} + \frac{4}{7}$	h	$\frac{5}{11} + \frac{2}{3}$	i	$\frac{2}{6} + \frac{3}{8}$	j	$\frac{1}{3} + \frac{6}{7}$

2 Write your answers to Question 1 as mixed numbers.

Example

$\frac{13}{9} = 1\frac{4}{9}$

Subtracting fractions

Subtract fractions with the same denominator and denominators that are multiples of the same number

Challenge 1

1 Subtract these fractions.

a $\frac{6}{8} - \frac{3}{8}$ b $\frac{7}{6} - \frac{2}{6}$ c $\frac{11}{10} - \frac{5}{10}$ d $\frac{5}{3} - \frac{2}{3}$

e $\frac{10}{7} - \frac{4}{7}$ f $\frac{12}{8} - \frac{7}{8}$ g $\frac{8}{5} - \frac{2}{5}$ h $\frac{7}{4} - \frac{2}{4}$

2 Write two different fraction subtractions for each answer.

a $\frac{3}{10}$ b $\frac{2}{8}$ c $\frac{4}{11}$ d $\frac{1}{7}$

e $\frac{3}{12}$ f $\frac{5}{13}$ g $\frac{4}{9}$ h $\frac{6}{12}$

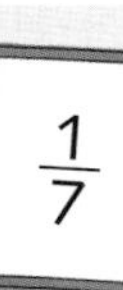

Example

$\frac{2}{7} = \frac{6}{7} - \frac{4}{7}$

$= \frac{5}{7} - \frac{3}{7}$

Challenge 2

1 Subtract these fractions.

a $\frac{14}{12} - \frac{3}{4}$ b $\frac{10}{8} - \frac{1}{2}$ c $\frac{14}{9} - \frac{2}{3}$ d $\frac{9}{5} - \frac{3}{10}$ e $\frac{5}{7} - \frac{4}{14}$ f $\frac{8}{5} - \frac{1}{4}$

g $\frac{7}{5} - \frac{1}{2}$ h $\frac{5}{3} - \frac{2}{6}$ i $\frac{6}{4} - \frac{1}{2}$ j $\frac{8}{6} - \frac{1}{3}$ k $\frac{7}{3} - \frac{3}{9}$ l $\frac{4}{2} - \frac{2}{6}$

2 Choose two of your answers from Question 1 and write them as mixed numbers.

Example

$\frac{11}{8} = 1\frac{3}{8}$

3 Work out these fraction problems.

a Joshua lives $1\frac{3}{8}$ miles from the school. Sylvia lives $\frac{1}{4}$ mile from the school. How much closer than Joshua is Sylvia to the school?

b A football player runs $\frac{2}{3}$ the length of the pitch. A second player in the same team runs $\frac{3}{4}$ the length of the pitch. What fraction more of the pitch did the second player run? If the pitch was 120 m long, how much further would he have run?

c A recipe needs $1\frac{3}{4}$ cups of flour and $\frac{4}{6}$ of a cup of sugar. How much more flour than sugar does the recipe need?

d My bottle of water contains $1\frac{1}{2}$ litres. I drink $\frac{3}{5}$ of a litre in the morning. What fraction is left?

Challenge 3

1 Subtract these fractions.

a $\frac{5}{2} - \frac{3}{9}$	**b** $\frac{12}{9} - \frac{3}{4}$	**c** $\frac{8}{5} - \frac{4}{7}$	**d** $\frac{9}{8} - \frac{2}{10}$
e $\frac{8}{6} - \frac{4}{5}$	**f** $\frac{4}{3} - \frac{5}{7}$	**g** $\frac{16}{10} - \frac{2}{3}$	**h** $\frac{13}{7} - \frac{4}{6}$
i $\frac{15}{8} - \frac{3}{4}$	**j** $\frac{9}{5} - \frac{3}{3}$	**k** $\frac{12}{9} - \frac{2}{5}$	**l** $\frac{11}{7} - \frac{1}{5}$
m $\frac{13}{10} - \frac{1}{4}$	**n** $\frac{9}{6} - \frac{3}{5}$	**o** $\frac{5}{3} - \frac{2}{5}$	**p** $\frac{5}{2} - \frac{2}{7}$

2 Write your answers to Question 1 as mixed numbers.

3 a A bottle of water contains $1\frac{6}{8}$ litres of water. In the morning Tom drank $\frac{5}{12}$ of it. In the afternoon Tom drank $\frac{1}{4}$ of it. Then he spilt $\frac{2}{6}$ of it. How much is left?

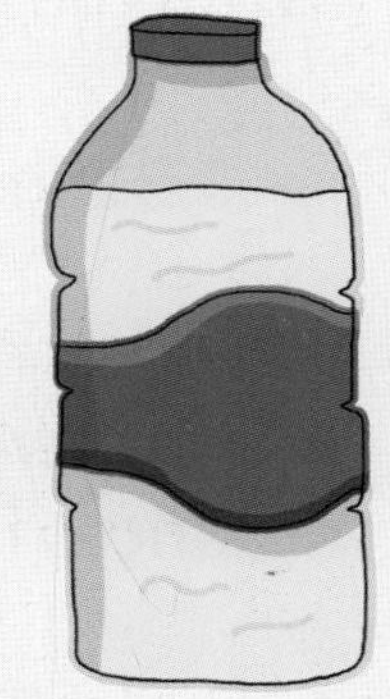

b Draw a diagram to show Tom's bottle of water and what happened to it all.

Converting lengths

Convert between kilometres and metres, centimetres and metres, and centimetres and millimetres

Each division on the rulers is 1 mm. Find the length of each nail.

Write your answer in: i millimetres ii centimetres

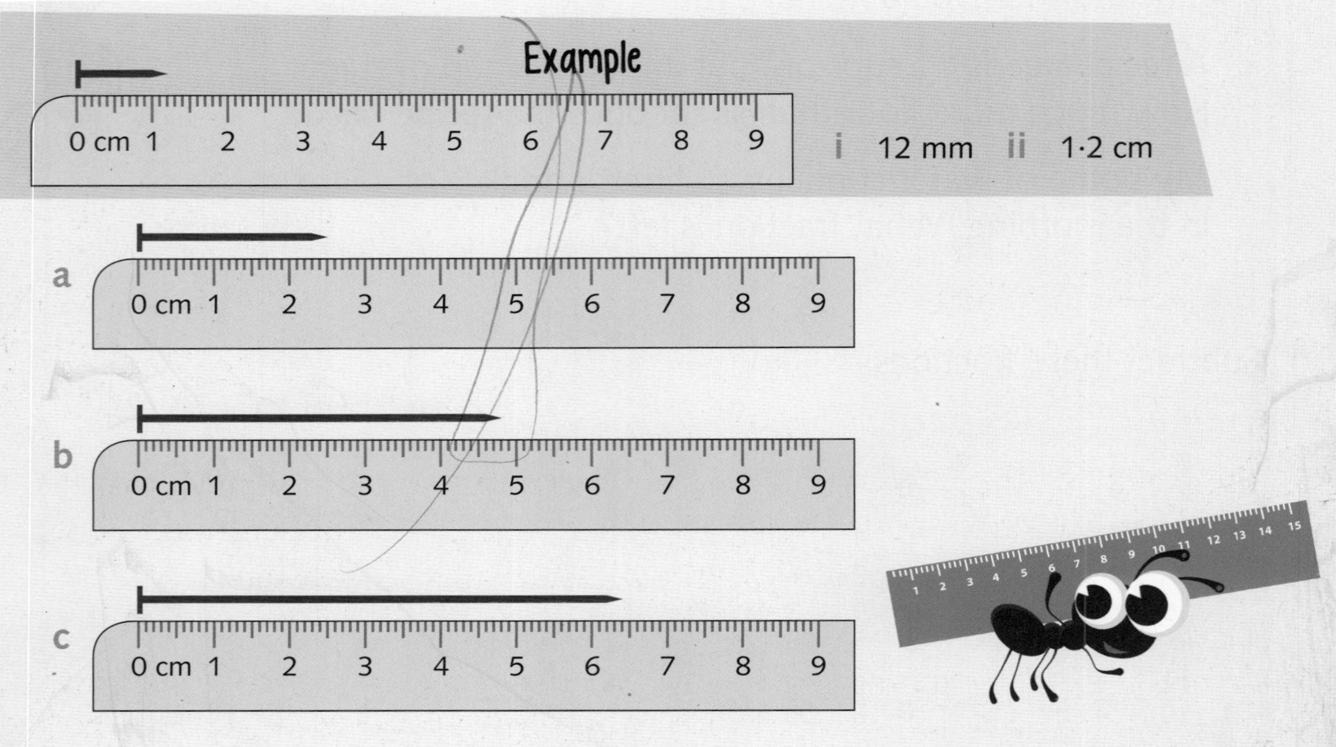

1 Write these distances in metres.

a 1·32 km b 0·53 km c 2·08 km d 3·82 km

2 A bus travelled the following distances. Write these distances in kilometres with 2 decimal places.

a 4170 m b 6090 m

c 12 570 m d 20 030 m

3 Write these lengths in metres using decimals.

a 750 cm b 640 cm c 2810 cm d 1360 mm e 990 mm f 1040 mm

4 The picture below shows the heights of five mountains.

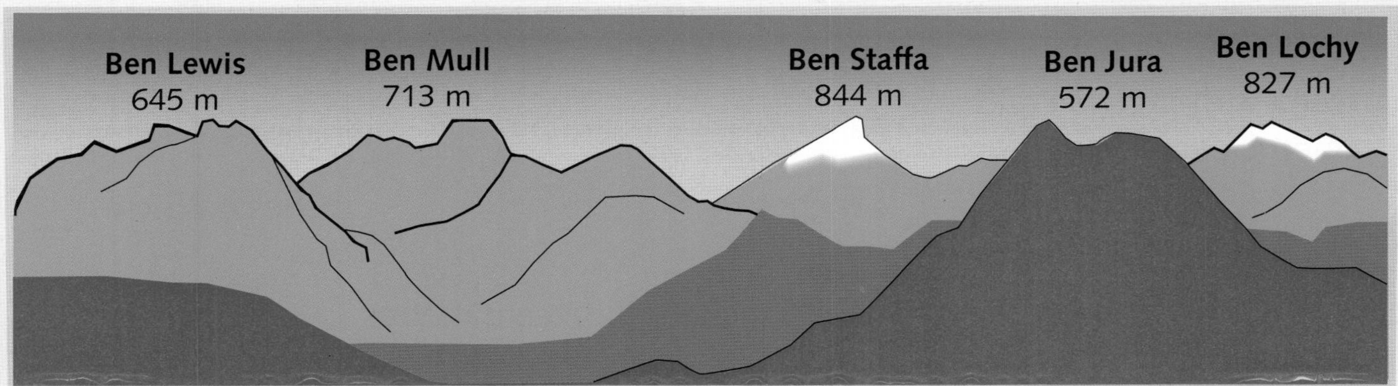

a Round the height of each mountain to the nearest 10 metres.

b Now write the height of each mountain in kilometres with 2 decimal places.

Example

Ben Muckle 791 m
791 m rounds to 790 m
790 m = 0·79 km

5 The picture of the five mountains is a view from the top of Ben Muckle. These are the distances from Ben Muckle to each of the other mountains. Write these distances in order. Start with the nearest mountain.

Ben Lewis	Ben Mull	Ben Staffa	Ben Jura	Ben Lochy
12·85 km	16 700 m	$19\frac{1}{2}$ km	10 820 m	21 km 50 m

Challenge 3

Amy and Lily reach the top of Ben Muckle. Amy writes down the height of the mountain in her log book, then adds a few lines of calculations.

Amy says, "I can make all the mountains that we can see the same height." Lily thinks this is nonsense.

Work out how Amy got from 791 to 1089 and then follow the same steps for the other mountains at the top of the page. What do you notice?

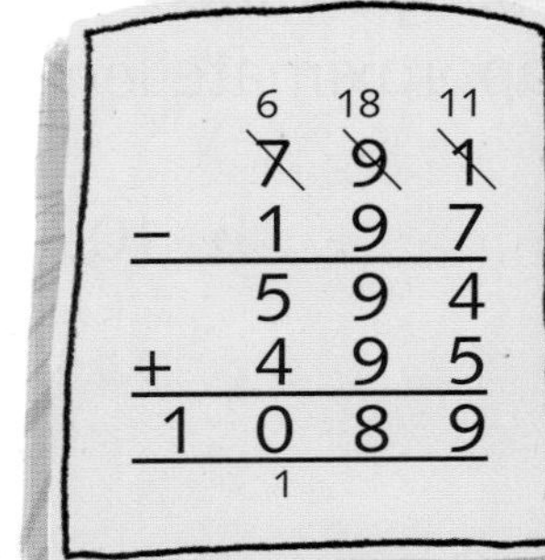

Hint

Look at the numbers in the calculations. Can you see what Amy has done?

Using metric and imperial units (2)

Know the imperial unit inch and the rough metric equivalent in centimetres

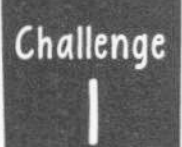

Challenge 1

1 Copy and complete the list of imperial and metric equivalences.

1 inch ≈ 2·5 cm

2 inches ≈ ☐ cm

4 inches ≈ ☐ cm

☐ inches ≈ 12·5 cm

☐ inches ≈ 15 cm

☐ inches ≈ 25 cm

2 Draw lines of these lengths. Write the length in centimetres above each line.

You will need:
- ruler

a 7·5 cm   b 10 cm   c 12·5 cm

3 Below each line you drew in Question 2 write its length in inches.

Challenge 2

1 Draw lines of these lengths. Write the length above each line.

You will need:
- ruler

a 15 cm   b 4 inches   c 17·5 cm   d 8 inches

e 20 cm   f 6 inches   g 100 mm   h 7 inches

2 Look at the lines that you drew in Question 1. Write which pairs are approximately equal in length.

Example

Line a (15 cm) ≈ line f (6 inches)

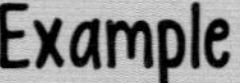

3 Use this relationship: 1 inch ≈ 2·5 cm.
Work out the approximate length in centimetres of these lines.

a 5 inches   b 10 inches   c 14 inches

d 12 inches   e 24 inches   f 36 inches

4 Compare the statements in each pair of speech bubbles then answer the questions.

a What is the height of the taller sunflower?

My marrow is 15 inches long.

My marrow is 40 cm long.

b What is the length of the longer marrow?

My rose bush is 130 cm high.

My rose bush is 50 inches high.

c Write the height of the taller bush.

My scarf is 48 inches long.

My scarf is 1 metre long.

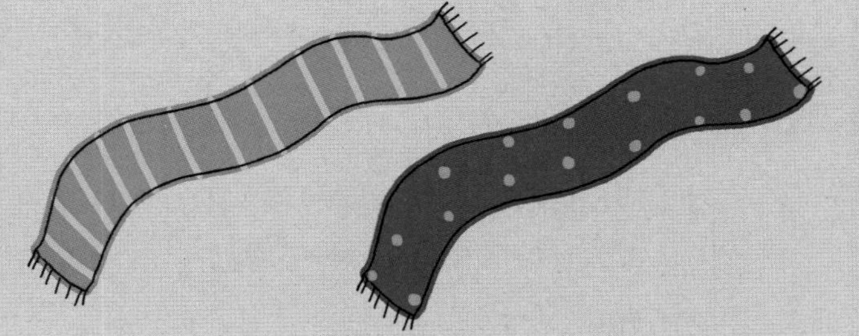

d What is the length of the longer scarf?

Challenge 3

1 Work out the diameter of the 1p coin.

2 If 1p coins are placed end to end to form a straight line, what is the value in pounds for lines of these lengths?

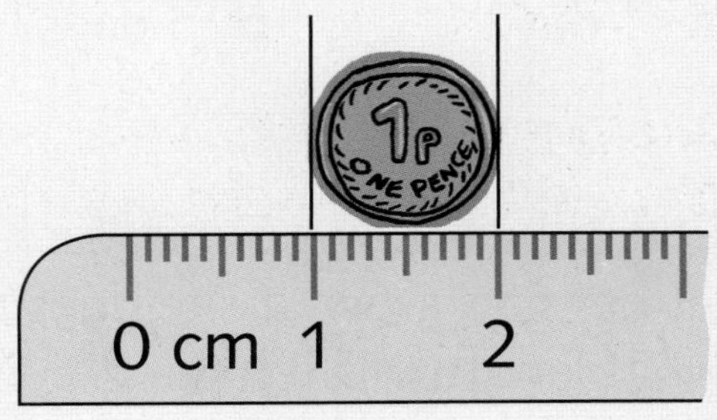

a 40 inches b 100 inches c 800 inches

Lengths and distances

Know which operation to use to solve problems involving length

Challenge 1

1 Write each set of lengths in order, starting with the shortest.

a 4 km 420 m, 4200 m, 4·5 km

b 3000 m, 3·5 km, 390 m

c 279 cm, 2·8 m, 2 m 8 cm

d 20 cm, 180 mm, 2·1 cm

2 Three children took part in the 'Welly Boot Throwing' competition at the school fair. Their results are shown in the table.

Name	Distance
Jacob	8·04 m
Lexie	8 m 16 cm
Martin	812 cm

a Who threw the wellington boot the furthest?

b How many centimetres was the winner's boot ahead of the runner up?

Challenge 2

1 Mrs Hassim lives 450 m from her shop.
How many kilometres does she walk to and from her shop in:

a 1 day? b 5 days?

2 Carla's hair grows 5 mm each week. She wants to let her hair grow. If she does not have it cut, what length will it have grown in:

a 4 weeks from now? b 1 year from now?

3 A Year 5 class measured how far their six snails could go in one hour.

a Write the snails' distances in order starting with the winning distance.

b How many centimetres separated the winning snail from:

i the snail that came second?

ii the snail that came fourth?

iii the snail that covered the least distance?

c How many centimetres ahead of Aggy was Lucky at the end of one hour?

Snail	Distance
Sammy	1216 cm
Nippy	12·18 m
Aggy	11 950 mm
Inky	11·83 m
Lucky	12.01 m
Skippy	1187 cm

4 An old snail is crawling towards the compost heap, which is 15 m away. In the first hour it crawled halfway towards the heap. In the next hour it crawled half of the remaining distance.

a How far did it travel in those two hours?

b How many centimetres does it still have to crawl?

c In the third hour it crawled about 1·97 m. How far does it still have to travel to reach the heap?

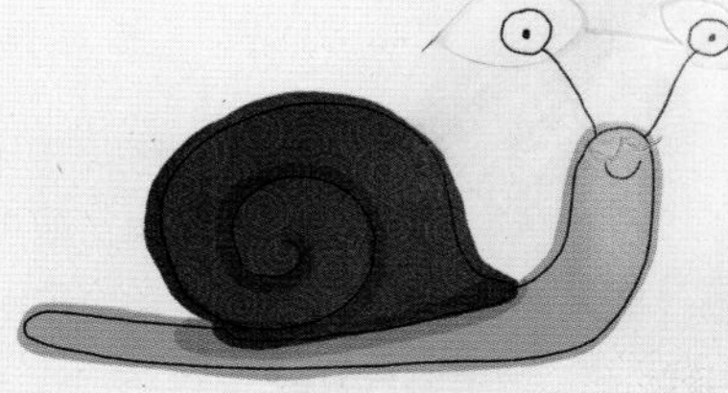

Challenge 3

You will need:

- 1 cm squared paper
- ruler
- coloured pencils

1 Draw this rectangular pattern on 1 cm squared paper so that each pair of lines is 1 cm apart. Begin with the smallest rectangle whose sides are 4 cm and 2 cm.

2 Make a table to record the perimeter of rectangles A, B and C.

3 Use the table to predict the perimeter of rectangles D and E in the pattern.

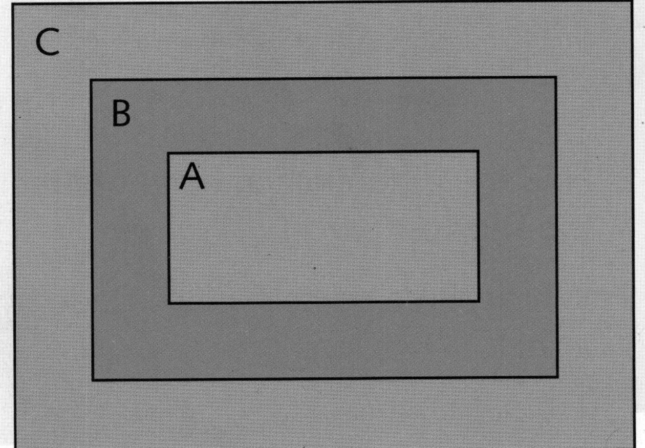

Multiple lengths

Know which operation to use to solve problems involving length and scaling

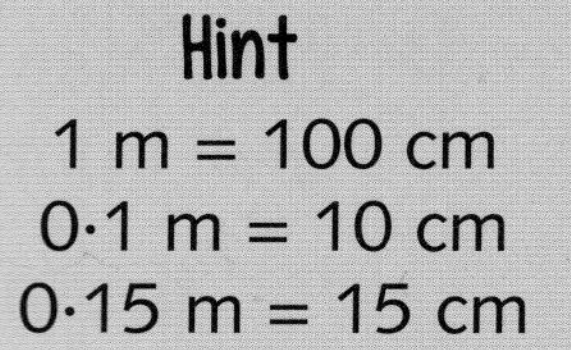

1 Write the length and height of each parcel in centimetres.

2 Find the difference in length between the parcels in metres.

3 Find the difference in height between the parcels in metres.

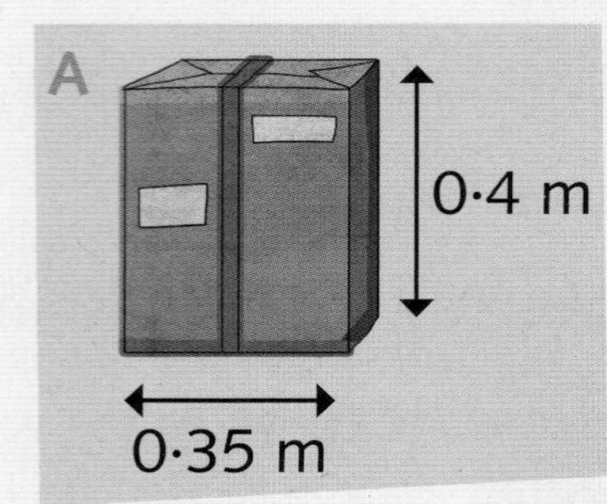

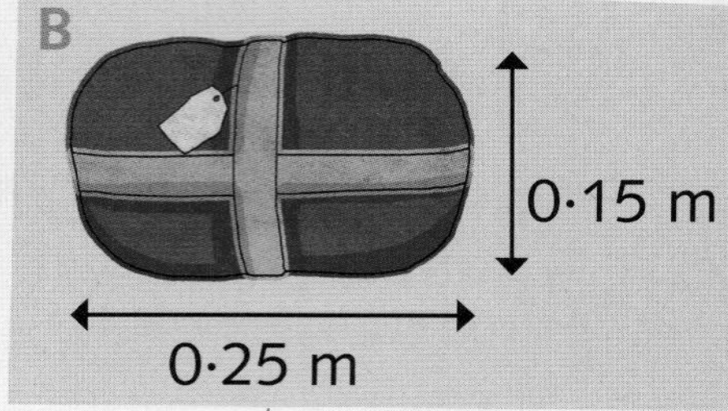

1 Write the length and height of each parcel in centimetres.

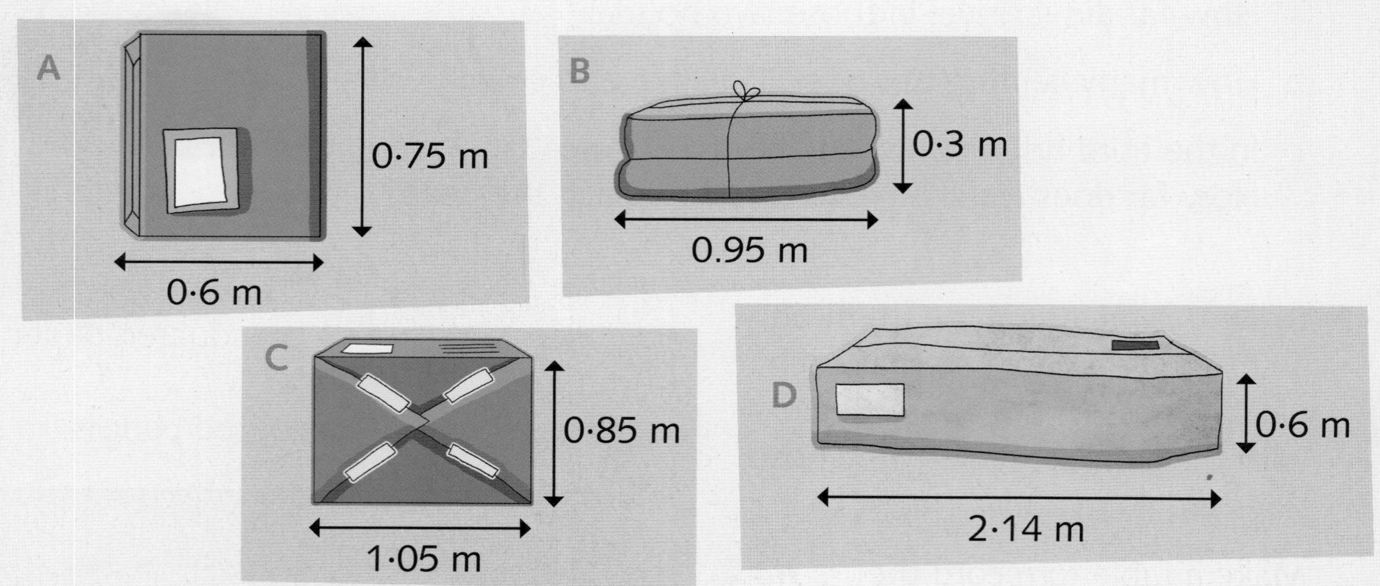

2 Find the difference in height in metres between the tallest and the shortest parcel.

3 Which three parcels, placed side by side with no gaps, will fit on to a shelf 3·7 m long?

4 In the warehouse, parcels identical to parcel D are stacked on top of one another. What is the total height of a stack of:

a 4 parcels?

b 8 parcels?

5 Craig bought these tiles to place above the sink in the bathroom. Work out in metres the tiled length of:

a a row of 5 tiles

b a column of 3 tiles

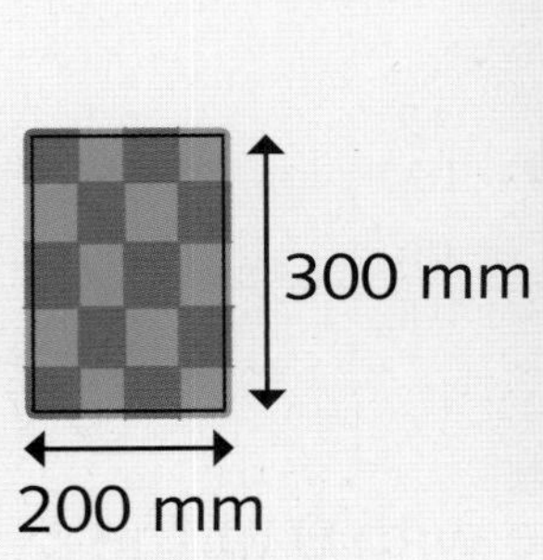

hallenge 3

1 The tile shop displays these rectangular patterns of tiles. Make a sketch of the next pattern and label it D.

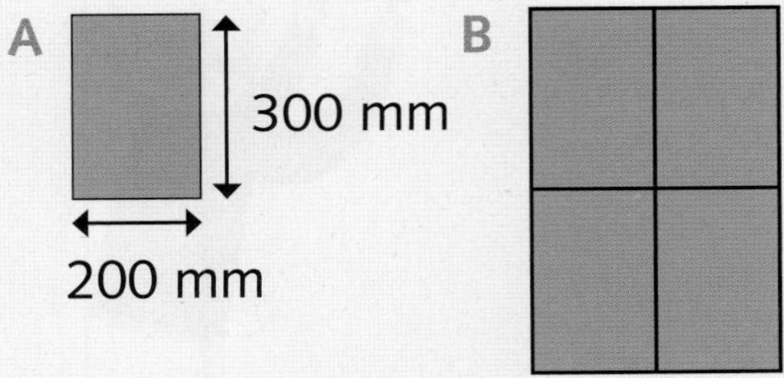

C

2 Copy and complete the table.

Pattern	**A**	**B**	**C**	**D**
Height of pattern (mm)				
Width of pattern (mm)				
Number of tiles				

3 What is the height and width of the pattern of tiles if you use:

a 25 tiles?

b 36 tiles?

Decimal thousandths

Recognise and use thousandths and relate them to tenths, hundredths and decimal equivalents

Challenge 1

1 Write the decimal fraction that is equivalent to these hundredths.

a $\frac{45}{100}$ b $\frac{12}{100}$ c $\frac{68}{100}$ d $\frac{29}{100}$

e $\frac{48}{100}$ f $\frac{99}{100}$ g $\frac{54}{100}$ h $\frac{7}{100}$

2 Draw a number line with 0 at the beginning and 1 at the end.
Put all your decimal answers from Question 1 on the number line.

0·45 goes near to 0·50, which is halfway.

0.45

0

1

Challenge 2

1 Write the decimal fraction that is equivalent to these thousandths.

a $\frac{461}{1000}$ b $\frac{102}{1000}$ c $\frac{834}{1000}$ d $\frac{529}{1000}$ e $\frac{903}{1000}$ f $\frac{255}{1000}$

g $\frac{989}{1000}$ h $\frac{384}{1000}$ i $\frac{136}{1000}$ j $\frac{842}{1000}$ k $\frac{937}{1000}$ l $\frac{736}{1000}$

2 Draw a number line with 0 at the beginning and 1 at the end.
Put all your decimal answers from Question 1 on the number line.

3 Write three decimal thousandths that could come between these decimals.

a 0 ——— 0·100

b 0·300 ——— 0·400

c 0·500 ——— 0·700

d 0·600 ——— 0·800

e 0·200 ——— 0·500

f 0·400 ——— 0·600

g 0·050 ——— 0·150

h 0·350 ——— 0·450

Challenge 3

1 Explain what thousandths are.

2 Write the decimal fraction that is equivalent to these thousandths.

a $\frac{11}{1000}$ b $\frac{9}{1000}$ c $\frac{78}{1000}$ d $\frac{1}{1000}$

e $\frac{6}{1000}$ f $\frac{99}{1000}$ g $\frac{45}{1000}$ h $\frac{61}{1000}$

i $\frac{124}{1000}$ j $\frac{283}{1000}$ k $\frac{111}{1000}$ l $\frac{406}{1000}$

3 Draw a number line with 0 at the beginning and 0·5 at the end.
Put all your decimal answers from Question 2 on the number line.

4 Jennie says that $\frac{54}{1000}$ is equal to 0·54.
Is she correct? Explain how you know.

Ordering thousandths

Read, write, order and compare numbers with up to 3 decimal places

Challenge 1

Count on in thousandths for five numbers from these decimals. Write your numbers as you count.

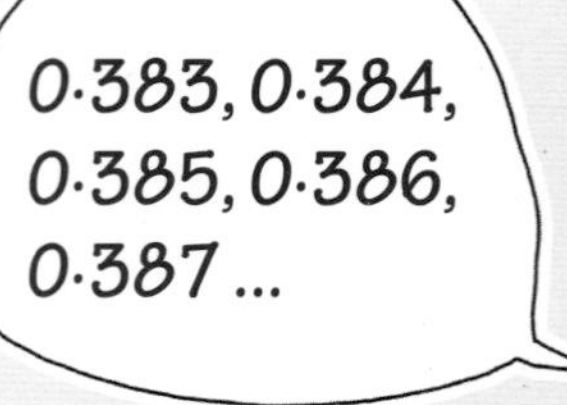

a 0·276	b 0·158	c 1·641
d 2·317	e 3·854	f 3·903
g 4·008	h 4·744	i 4·078
j 5·835	k 6·038	l 7·934

Challenge 2

1 Put these decimal numbers in order, smallest to largest.

a	0·863,	0·386,	0·286,	0·482,	0·183,	0·589
b	1·262,	1·082,	1·629,	1·148,	1·002,	1·735
c	2·761,	2·007,	2·629,	2·812,	2·529,	2·721
d	5·398,	5·981,	5·273,	5·286,	5·297,	5·101
e	4·387,	4·361,	4·308,	4·392,	4·343,	4·309
f	7·287,	7·629,	7·291,	7·602,	7·215,	7·659
g	8·911,	8·683,	8·827,	8·216,	8·825,	8·206
h	9·721,	9·377,	9·018,	9·726,	9·354,	9·013
i	6·675,	6·756,	6·075,	6·757,	6·005,	6·555
j	3·211,	3·121,	3·021,	3·102,	3·222,	3·011

2 Write the decimal numbers that are one thousandth smaller and one thousandth larger than each of these numbers.

a 2·387	b 3·209	c 5·114	d 6·804
e 1·055	f 7·852	g 6·255	h 8·888
i 9·005	j 8·078	k 7·045	l 8·617
m 5·299	n 7·301	o 8·001	p 3·333

allenge 3

1 Use the greater than > or less than < sign to make each statement correct.

a 2·645 ☐ 2·821	b 4·831 ☐ 4·762
c 5·558 ☐ 5·539	d 7·028 ☐ 7·038
e 8·156 ☐ 8·172	f 9·628 ☐ 9·691
g 6·529 ☐ 6·527	h 3·877 ☐ 3·866
i 4·003 ☐ 4·001	j 6·937 ☐ 6·973
k 1·626 ☐ 1·627	l 9·999 ☐ 9·909

2 Write some step-by-step instructions for ordering decimals to 3 places. Once you have written them, test them out to see if they work!

Rounding and ordering

- Read, write, order and compare numbers with up to 3 decimal places
- Round decimals with 2 decimal places to the nearest whole number and to 1 decimal place

1 Round these hundredths to the nearest whole number. You could use a number line to help you.

a 7·61 b 5·72 c 9·14 d 1·96

e 3·55 f 5·39 g 6·87 h 2·46

I know 4·26 rounds down to 4 and 4·83 rounds up to 5.

2 Put these thousandths in order, smallest to largest.

a 1·873, 1·265, 1·326, 1·587

b 4·615, 4·972, 4·355, 4·738

c 6·478, 6·013, 6·592, 6·308

d 2·198, 2·062, 2·643, 2·465

e 5·752, 5·391, 5·408, 5·635

f 3·992, 3·442, 3·881, 3·117

1 Draw a table like the one shown with a total of 13 rows. Write the numbers below in the middle column. Round the numbers to the nearest tenth and whole number. The first two have been done for you.

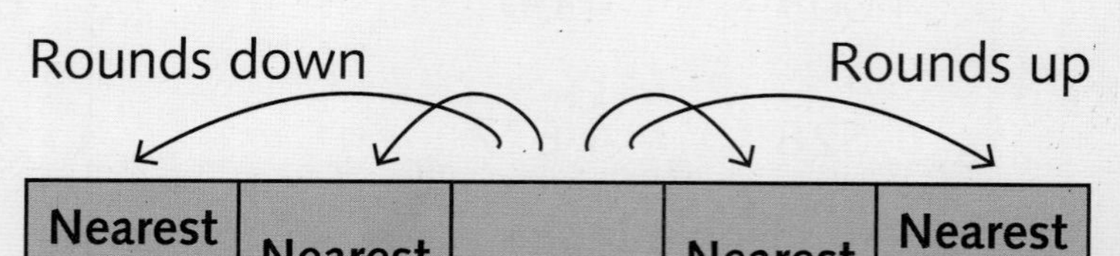

Nearest whole number	Nearest tenth	Number	Nearest tenth	Nearest whole number
3	3·2	3·21		
5		5·36	5·4	
		4·78		

a 3·21 b 5·36 c 4·78 d 8·92 e 1·45 f 7·51

g 6·98 h 9·08 i 5·34 j 2·72 k 6·15 l 7·89

2 Put these thousandths in order, smallest to largest.

a 2·762, 2·812, 2·081, 2·315, 2·852, 2·301

b 5·926, 5·222, 5·817, 5·133, 5·562, 5·001

c 4·018, 4·003, 4·081, 4·088, 4·011, 4·013

d 7·987, 7·879, 7·998, 7·898, 7·997, 7·888

e 3·252, 2·522, 2·555, 2·525, 2·552, 2·225

f 8·126, 8·129, 8·012, 8·029, 8·192, 8·012

3 Add one thousandth to each of these numbers.

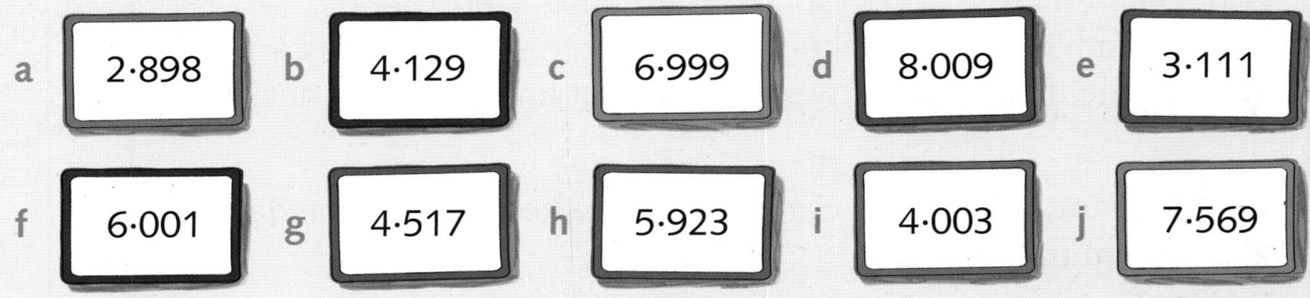

hallenge 3

1 Explain how to round decimal numbers with 2 places to the nearest decimal with 1 place.

2 Write these decimal numbers in order, smallest to largest.

a 6·962, 6·262, 6·002, 6·669, 6·609, 6·996

b 2·872, 2·83, 2·982, 2·91, 2·992, 2·19

c 4·3, 4·35, 4·03, 4·55, 4·5, 4·05

d 7·265, 7·26, 7·65, 7·652, 7·625, 7·62

e 0·37, 0·3, 0·73, 0·7, 0·77, 0·33

f 5·005, 5·05, 5·5, 5·505, 5·015, 5·1

Decimal problems

Solve problems involving decimals

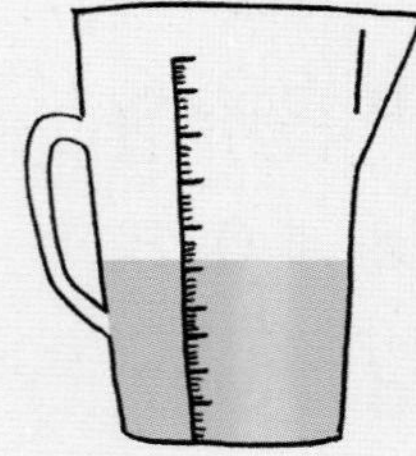

Challenge 1

1 Year 5 have been measuring weekly rainfall.

a In the first week the rain gauge showed 0·028 m and in the second week it showed 0·037 m. What was the total rainfall for those two weeks?

b Year 5 had predicted that the total rainfall for three weeks would be 0·095 m. How much rain needed to fall in the third week to make their prediction correct?

2 Four children ran a 200 m sprint. Their times were: 34·2 s, 31·72 s, 34·52 s and 33·15 s. Put them in order from slowest to fastest. What is the difference between the fastest and slowest times?

3 On a walking holiday the Carter family walked 4·7 km one day and 3·5 km the next day.

a How far did they walk in total?

b By the end of the third day they had walked 11 km. How far did they walk on day three?

4 Joe goes to the cheese shop and buys two packs of cheese. One costs £3.65. He pays with a £10 note and receives £2.35 change. How much did the second pack of cheese cost?

Challenge 2

1 The table shows Year 5's predictions for the next three weeks' rainfall.

a What do they think the total rainfall is going to be?

b What is the difference between the rainfall for the wettest week and the rainfall for the driest week?

c The actual rainfall for the three weeks was 0·204 m. How much more than their prediction was this?

Week	Rainfall (metres)
Week 1:	0·065
Week 2:	0·039
Week 3:	0·047

2 Four children do the 200 m sprint.
Their times are: 35·84 s, 31·2 s, 30·76 s and 29·53 s.

a What is the difference between the slowest time and the fastest time?

b If the children all ran a 4 × 200 m relay together, what would their total time be?

3 Amina walks 2·762 km every day. How far does she walk in five days?

4 Joe buys a total of 1·638 kg of cheese. 0·855 kg is Cheddar, and the rest is blue cheese. How much does the blue cheese weigh?

5 Work in a group of four.

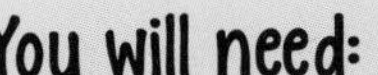

- digital stopwatch that uses hundredths of a second

- Time how long it takes each of you to jump up and down 20 times.
- Record all your times and put them in order.
- Work out the difference in time between the fastest and the slowest.
- Time one another again. How much did your times change by?

1 Year 5 have been measuring weekly rainfall for the last three weeks. The total rainfall was 0·265 m. In week one 0·09 m fell and in week two 0·05 m fell. How much fell in week three?

2 Sam has been recording his times for the 200 m sprint.
His times are 37·9 s, 37·09 s, 37·29 s and 37·95 s.

a Put his times in order, slowest to fastest.

b What is the difference between his slowest time and his fastest time?

c His target is 36·5 s. How much does he need to improve by?

3 On a long journey the Jones family drive 56·382 km before lunch and 68·314 km after lunch. The sat nav told them the journey would be 178·65 km in total. How much further have they got to travel?

4 Rosie buys some cheese. It weighs 2·275 kg. 1·2 kg is Red Leicester and the rest is Cheddar. How much Cheddar does she have? When she gets home her mum is making cheese sauce and uses 80 g of Cheddar. How much is left?

Adding decimals

Add decimals with 1 and 2 decimal places mentally

1 Add these decimals with 1 decimal place. Show your working out.

a 0·3 + 0·5 b 0·6 + 0·2 c 0·4 + 0·4 d 0·7 + 0·5

e 0·6 + 0·8 f 0·9 + 0·6 g 0·7 + 0·7 h 0·9 + 0·8

2 Add these decimals with 2 decimal places. Show your working out.

a 0·26 + 0·31 b 0·35 + 0·18 c 0·46 + 0·27 d 0·38 + 0·45

e 0·52 + 0·36 f 0·27 + 0·65 g 0·71 + 0·16 h 0·83 + 0·06

1 Play with a partner.

- Take turns to roll the two 0–9 dice.
- Read the numbers rolled as decimals with 1 decimal place. So if you roll 3 and 8, your numbers will be 0·3 and 0·8.
- Add the decimals together mentally.
- If the answer is on the grid cover it with a counter.

The first player to have three counters in any row, column or diagonal line is the winner.

You will need:
- 2 × 0–9 dice
- 20 counters in two different colours (ten of the same colour for each player)

0·8	0·7	0·8	0·9	0·6	1·6	0·9
1·1	0·2	0·5	1·2	0·4	1·3	1·7
1·7	1·3	0·8	0·5	0·6	1·5	1·1
0·3	0·2	0·9	0·4	1·1	0·8	0·7
1·8	1·4	1	1·4	0·4	1·2	1·6
0·6	0·4	1·4	0·7	0·3	1·3	0
1·5	1	1·2	0·1	1	0·7	0·2

2 Add these numbers. Show your working out.

a 0·46 + 0·73 b 0·68 + 0·55 c 0·79 + 0·36 d 0·84 + 0·28

e 0·47 + 0·53 f 0·93 + 0·22 g 0·85 + 0·76 h 0·74 + 0·65

3 How many different ways can you complete this calculation using the number cards below? Work out the answer to each of your calculations.

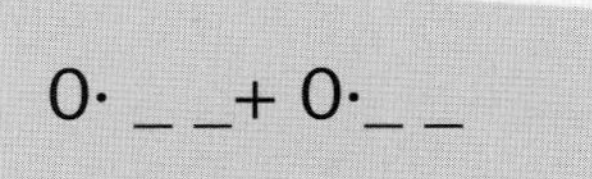

2 4 7 9

- Compare your totals with a partner.
- Have either of you found any your partner has not?
- Work together to organise your calculations in a systematic way.

Challenge 3

1 Explain how known facts can be used to add decimals.

2 For each of these answers write two different decimal additions.

a 1·76 b 1·82 c 1·45 d 1·07 e 1·52

f 1·38 g 1·12 h 1·49 i 1·65 j 1·02

Subtracting decimals

Subtract decimals with 1 and 2 decimal places mentally

Challenge 1

1 Subtract these decimals with 1 decimal place. Show your working out.

a 0·7 – 0·5 b 0·8 – 0·2 c 0·9 – 0·4 d 0·8 – 0·1

e 0·7 – 0·3 f 1·2 – 0·5 g 1·4 – 0·6 h 1·5 – 0·7

2 Subtract these decimals with 2 decimal places. Show your working out.

a 0·65 – 0·43 b 0·54 – 0·42 c 0·72 – 0·33 d 0·59 – 0·14

e 0·68 – 0·39 f 0·96 – 0·28 g 0·74 – 0·37 h 0·85 – 0·46

Challenge 2

1 For each of these answers write two different decimal subtractions.

a 0·6 b 0·9 c 0·4

d 0·5 e 0·7 f 0·2

2 Subtract these decimal numbers. Show your working out.

a 1·38 – 0·52 b 1·44 – 0·76 c 1·25 – 0·51 d 1·72 – 0·93

e 1·06 – 0·39 f 1·51 – 0·84 g 1·16 – 0·73 h 1·62 – 0·48

3 How many different ways can you complete this calculation using the number cards below? Work out the answer to each of your calculations.

7

0·_ _ – 0·_ _

- Compare your totals with a partner.
- Have either of you found any your partner has not?
- Work together to organise your calculations in a systematic way.

Challenge 3

1 For each of these answers write two different decimal subtractions.

a 

b 1·82

c 

d 

e 

f 1·38 g 0·32 h 0·88 i 0·15 j 0·43

2 Complete the calculations. Show your working out.

a 1·65 – ★ = 0·88	b 1·38 – ★ = 0·27	c 1·42 – ★ = 0·64
d 1·47 – ★ = 0·91	e 1·05 – ★ = 0·75	f ★ – 0·65 = 0·79
g ★ – 0·25 = 0·94	h ★ – 0·81 = 0·63	i ★ – 0·59 = 0·87
j ★ – 0·67 = 0·69	k 2·48 – ★ = 0·81	l ★ – 1·85 = 1·79

3 Work out the calculation chain below starting from each of these numbers.

a 1·54	b 1·62	c 1·81	d 1·97
e 1·75	f 1·66	g 1·89	h 1·73

Finish number ← ?  ?  ?  ?  Start number

–0·37 –0·28 –0·05 –0·43 –0·16

Whole number and decimal calculations

Add and subtract a mix of whole numbers and decimals

Challenge 1

1 Add these decimals with 1 decimal place. Show your working out.

a 3·5 + 4·3 b 2·7 + 5·1 c 6·2 + 2·7 d 5·8 + 3·6

e 4·9 + 3·2 f 6·5 + 4·7 g 7·8 + 5·5 h 8·7 + 4·3

2 Subtract these decimals with 1 decimal place. Show your working out.

a 7·6 – 2·3 b 6·8 – 4·5 c 7·9 – 4·1 d 5·3 – 2·5

e 6·7 – 3·8 f 4·5 – 1·7 g 7·1 – 3·5 h 8·3 – 4·6

Challenge 2

1 Choose numbers from these squares and write five addition and five subtraction calculations. Work out the answers. Show your working out.

2 Choose numbers from these squares and write ten addition calculations. Work out the answers. Show your working out.

3 Write two addition and two subtraction calculations to go with these trios.

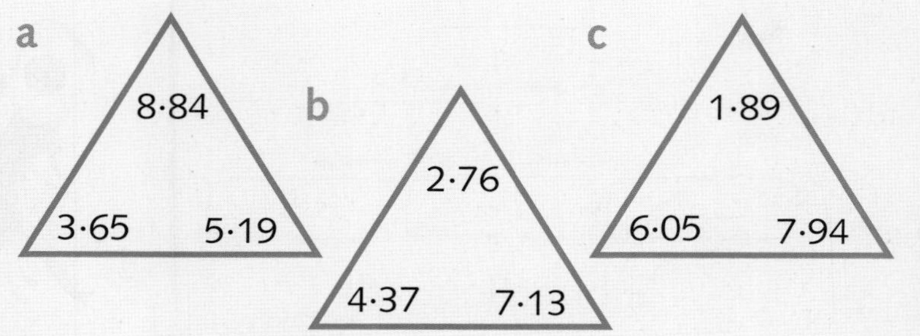

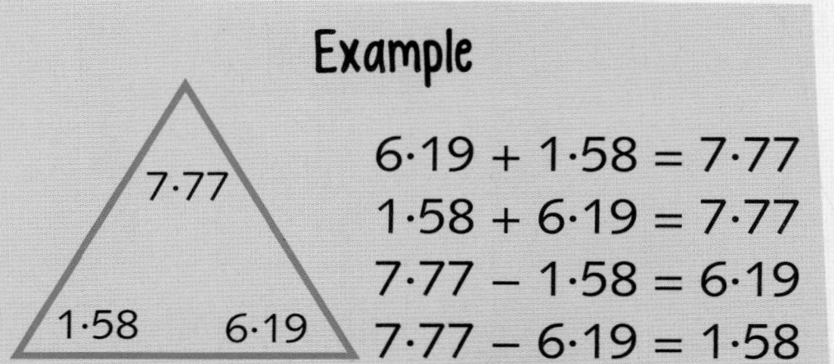

4 Fill in the missing numbers on these trios. There are two possible answers for each one.

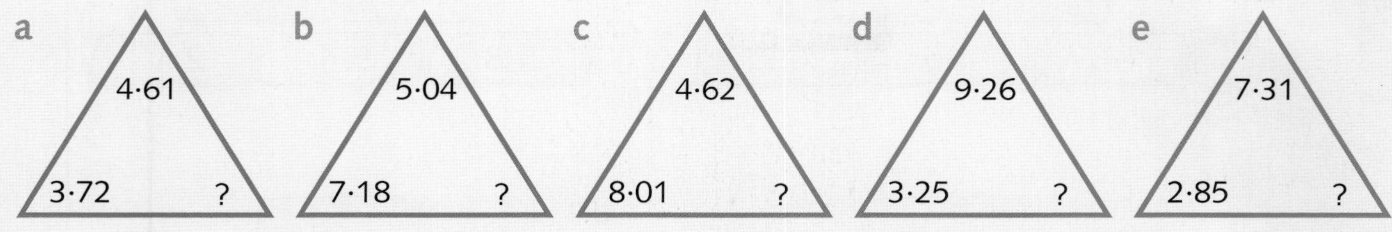

Challenge 2

Complete the calculations. Show your working out.

a 3·67 – ☆ = 9·58

b 4·83 + ☆ = 13·27

c 12·99 + ☆ = 17·63

d 23·52 – ☆ = 18·81

e 19·37 – ☆ = 15·07

f ☆ + 3·71 = 16·02

g ☆ + 9·23 = 14·86

h ☆ – 5·83 = 15·26

i ☆ – 14·28 = 19·53

j ☆ + 17·83 = 21·01

Decimal walls

Add and subtract decimals with different numbers of decimal places

Challenge 1

Copy and complete each decimal wall twice, first adding the numbers and then subtracting them.

Example

Addition wall

	23·4	
9·3	14·1	
3·7	5·6	8·5

Subtraction wall

	1	
1·9	2·9	
3·7	5·6	8·5

a 1·6, 4·5, 6·7

b 5·8, 9·4, 2·1

c 2·7, 7·3, 6·5

d 3·7, 9·1, 6·6

e 8·4, 11·7, 13·8

f 18·3, 14·8, 11·4

hallenge 2

Copy and complete the decimal walls. When you work out the bottom row, include some decimals with 1 decimal place and some decimals with 2 decimal places. Use subtraction to work out the bottom row and addition to work out the top two rows.

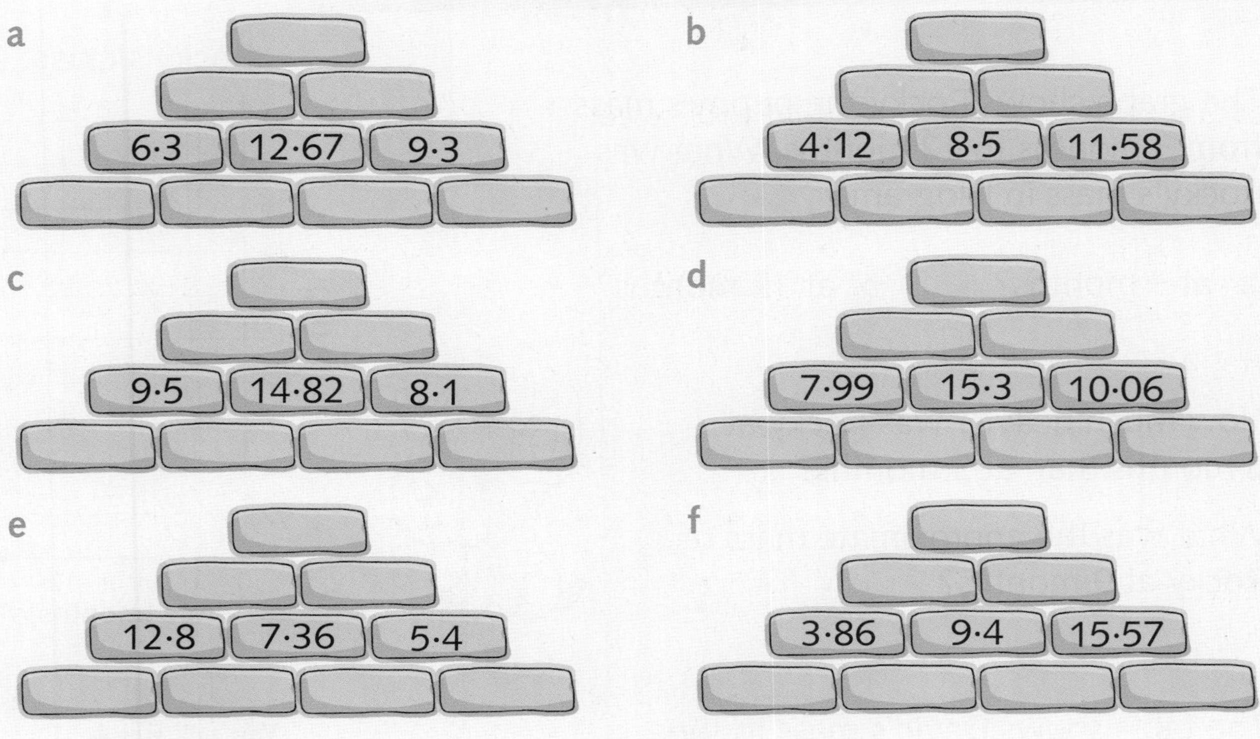

hallenge 3

Copy and complete the decimal walls. When you work out the bottom row, include at least one decimal with 1 decimal place, one decimal with 2 decimal places and one decimal with 3 decimal places. Use subtraction to work out the bottom row and addition to work out the top two rows.

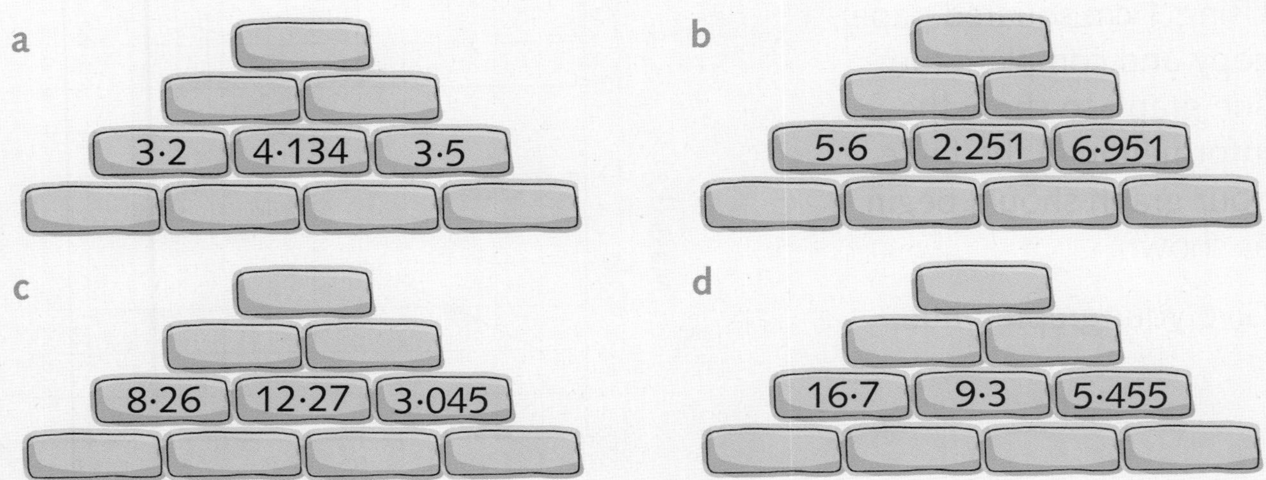

Growing up line graphs

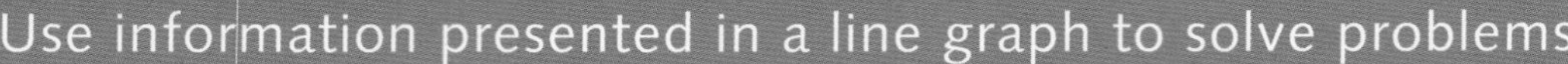

Use information presented in a line graph to solve problems

Challenge 1

1 The graph shows Rocky the puppy's mass from 3 months to 12 months. What was Rocky's mass in kilograms:

a at 3 months? b at 12 months?

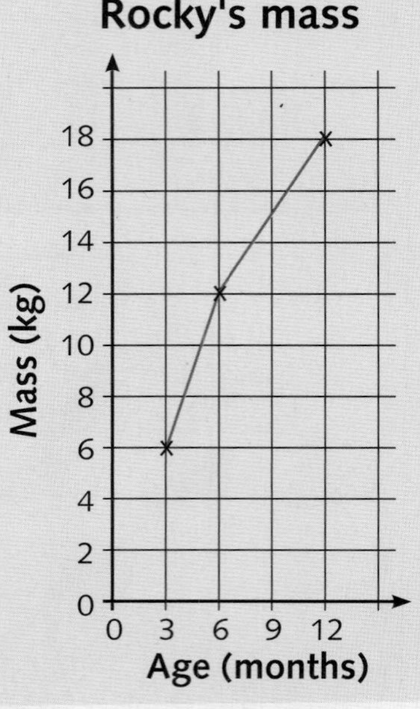

2 How much heavier was Rocky at 6 months than at 3 months?

3 What was the approximate mass of Rocky at 9 months?

Challenge 2

1 The table shows David's mass to the nearest kilogram from the age of 1 to 17.

Age (years)	1	3	5	7	9	11	13	15	17
Mass (kg)	12	15	20	25	30	35	50	55	65

You will need:

- 1 cm squared paper
- ruler

- Using 1 cm squared paper, copy and complete the line graph to show the information in the table. Your graph should begin as shown.
- Give your graph a title.

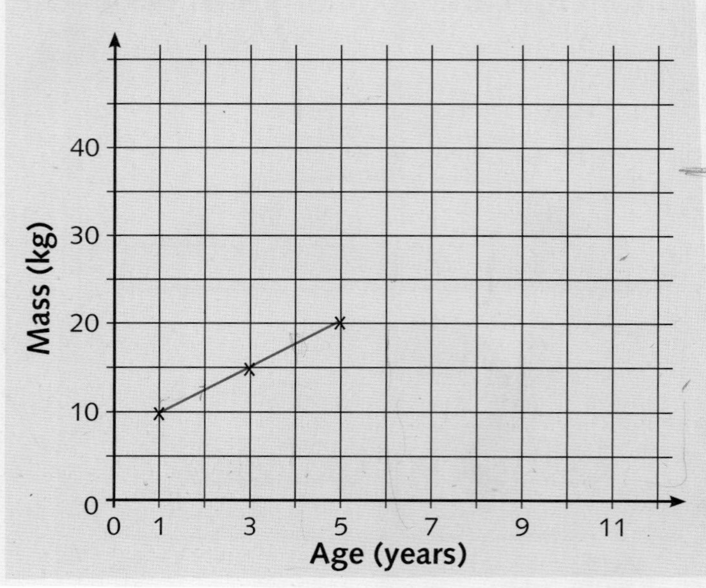

2 Between which ages did David's mass increase most quickly?

3 Use your graph to find David's approximate mass at these ages.

a 16 years b 14 years c 12 years d 10 years

e 8 years f 6 years g 4 years h 2 years

4 What was the difference in David's mass between the ages of:

a 5 and 10 years? b 10 and 15 years?

5 How many more kilograms did David gain between the ages of 10 and 15 years than between the ages of 5 and 10 years?

Challenge 3

1 The graph shows David's height measured in centimetres from the age of 9 to 17. What did David's height measure:

a at age 10?

b at age 14?

2 Between which ages did he gain 7·5 cm in height?

3 About how old was he when he measured 165 cm?

4 Use the information in the graph to write two different statements about David's height.

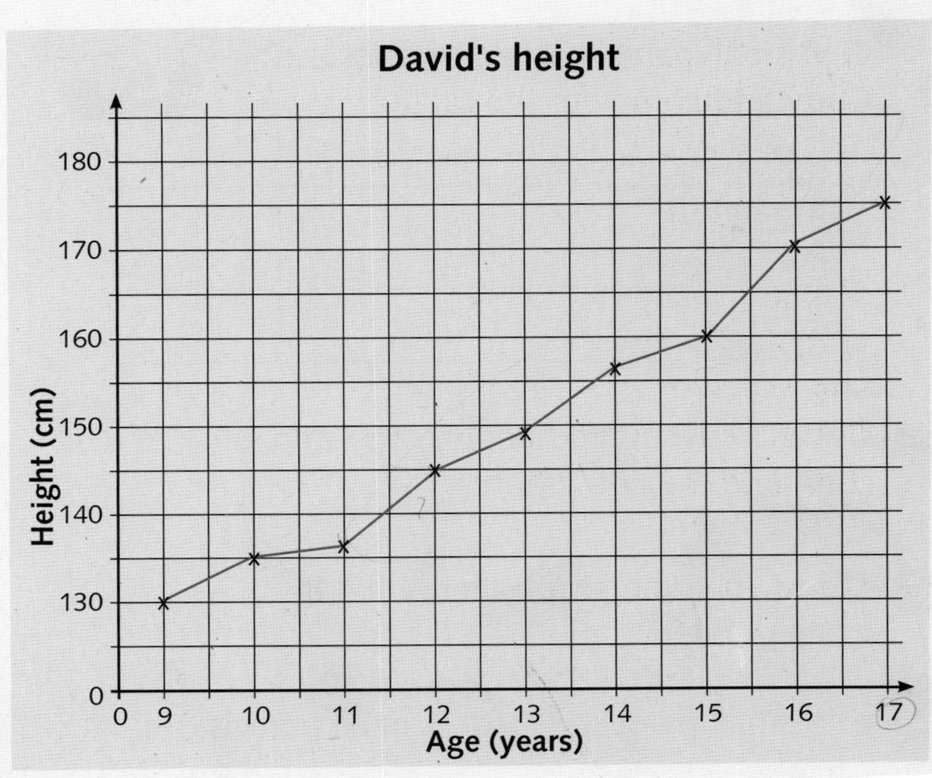

Post office straight line graphs

Use information presented in a line graph to solve problems

1 A Second Class stamp costs 50p. Copy and complete the table.

You will need:
- 1 cm squared paper
- ruler

Number of stamps	1	2	3	4	5	6
Cost (p)	50	100				

2 Using 1 cm squared paper, copy and complete the line graph.

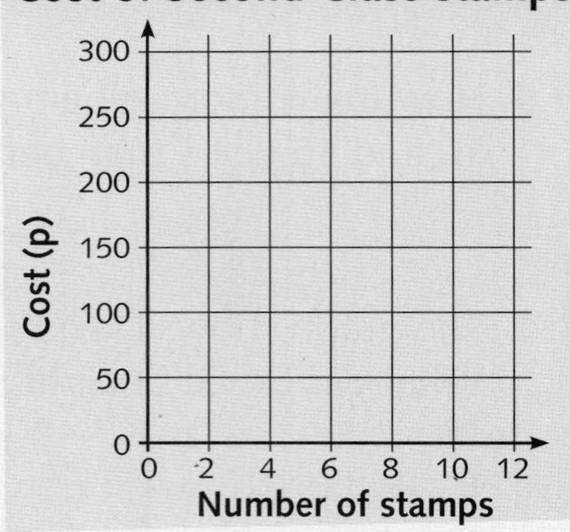

3 How many Second Class stamps can you buy for:

a £2.50? b £5?

1 One small parcel costs £3 to post. Copy and complete the table.

You will need:
- 1 cm squared paper
- ruler

Number of small parcels	2	4	6	8	10	12
Cost (£)	6	12				

2 Using 1 cm squared paper, copy and complete the line graph.

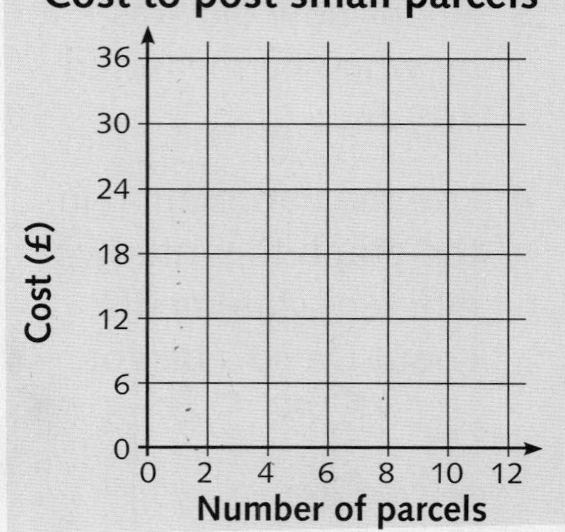

3 Using your line graph, find what it costs to post:

a 5 small parcels b 9 small parcels

4 How many small parcels can you post for:

a £33? b £21?

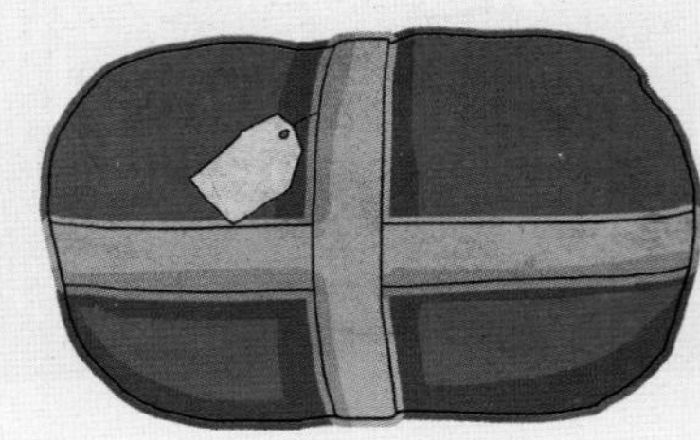

5 What will it cost to post:

a 30 small parcels? b 100 small parcels?

6 What is the total cost of postage for the small parcels in Question 5?

7 Find the difference in postage costs for 48 small parcels and 62 small parcels.

1 Tom is going on holiday to the United States. He bought his dollars at the post office. Using the rate of exchange £1 = \$1.50, copy and complete the table.

You will need:
- 1 cm squared paper
- ruler

Pounds (£)	20	40	60	80	100	120
Dollars (\$)	30					

2 a Using 1 cm squared paper, copy and complete the line graph for converting pounds to dollars. Your graph should begin as shown below.

b Extend your line graph up to £200.

3 Use your line graph to answer these questions.

a Convert these pounds to the nearest dollar.

i £140 ii £200

iii £160 iv £50

b Convert these dollars to the nearest pound.

i \$120 ii \$180

iii \$150 iv \$270

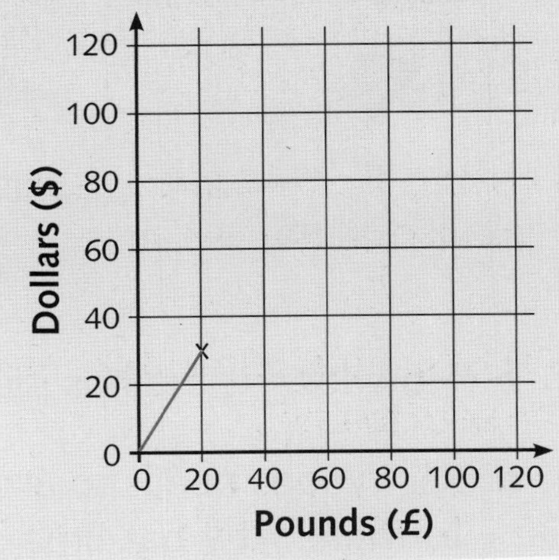

Data in tables and timetables

Complete, read and interpret data in tables and timetables

A bus leaves Market Street Bus Station in the town and travels to these villages. The journey time between each village is 10 minutes.

a Copy and complete the bus timetable.

Bus stop	Arrival time		
Market Street	10:15		
Northford	10:25		
Easton	10:35	10:55	
Southam			
Westerby			11:35

b How long is the journey from Market Street Bus Station to the bus stop in Westerby?

1 This is part of a bus timetable from Cambridge to Luton Airport.

a Copy and complete the timetable for the 12:30, 14:00 and 15:30 buses.

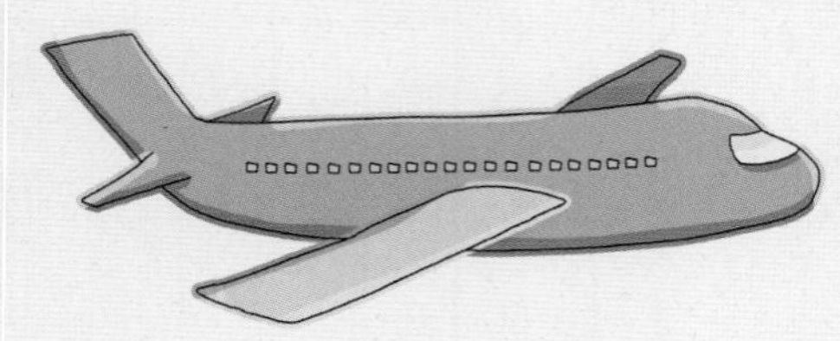

Bus stop	Arrival time			
Cambridge	11:00	12:30	14:00	15:30
Harston	11:15	12:45		
Royston	11:25			
Letchworth	11:42			
Hitchin	11:50			
Luton Airport	12:05	13:35	15:05	16:35

b How long is the bus journey from Royston to Luton Airport?

c Mr Woods needs to arrive at Luton Airport no later than quarter to three. At what time does he need to board the bus at Letchworth?

2 Several airlines fly from Luton to Palma. The table shows the flight times and costs.

Flight number	Departs	Arrives	Cost (£)
BR 0291	06:20	09:40	189
RZ 0357	10:40	14:25	194
BR 0295	12:35	16:00	199
JE 1426	14:55	18:25	180
IT 1155	17:05	20:30	165

a Which flight to Palma is the cheapest and how long does the flight take?

b Which of the two BR flights has the shorter flying time and by how many minutes?

c Ros arrived in Palma at 2:25 p.m. What was the cost of her ticket?

d Liam paid £180 for his ticket. At what time did his flight depart from Luton?

hallenge 3

This table shows some of the train times from Kings Cross Station in London to Luton Airport.

Train station	Arrival time					
Kings Cross Station	16:01	16:16	16:19	16:34	16:46	17:04
Luton Airport	16:31	16:46	17:02	17:04	17:16	17:37

a The express train takes exactly 30 minutes for the journey. Which of the above times from Kings Cross Station are for express trains?

b A passenger takes the 16:19 train. How long is the journey to Luton Airport in minutes?

c At what time does the slowest train to Luton Airport leave from Kings Cross Station?

d A family have tickets for a flight departing from Luton Airport at 19:35. They must allow 15 minutes for the shuttle bus service from the station at Luton to the airport and they must check in two hours before departure. Which train should they board at Kings Cross Station?

On the move

Use coordinates and scales to interpret information in time graphs

You will need:

- 1 cm squared paper
- ruler

1 This table shows the time and distance for a van driver's journey from the depot to a customer and back to the depot.

Copy and complete the time graph.

Time (minutes)	Distance (miles)
0	0
10	6
20	10
25	14
35	14
50	8
60	0

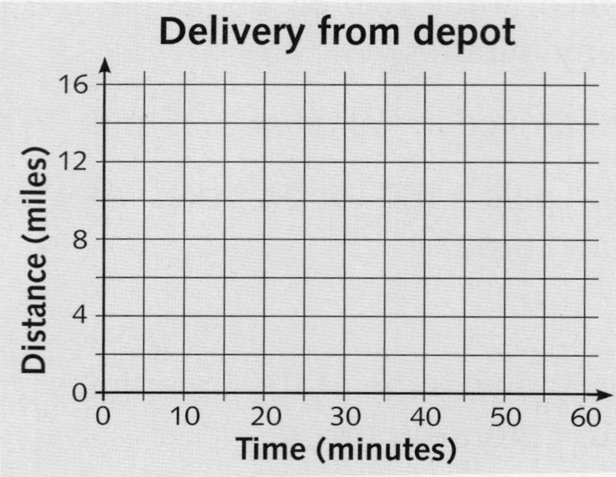

2 How many miles from the customer was the van driver at these times?

a 15 minutes b 20 minutes c 50 minutes d 55 minutes

1 The graph shows Mr Kerr's out and return journey from home to the airport to collect his son. How many miles from the airport was Mr Kerr at these times?

a 10 minutes

b 20 minutes

c 23 minutes

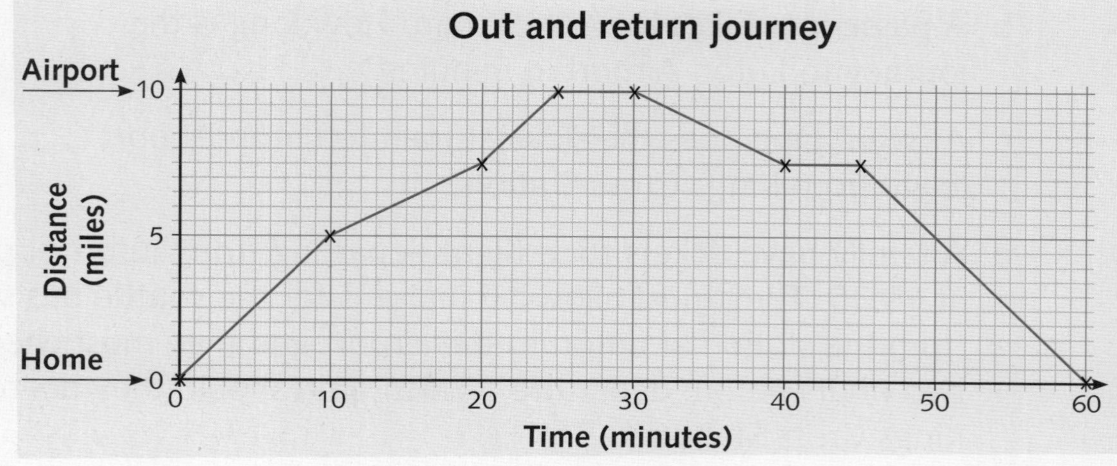

2 How many miles from home was Mr Kerr at these times?

a 45 minutes b 50 minutes c 54 minutes

3 How many minutes did it take Mr Kerr to drive to the airport?

4 For how many minutes was Mr Kerr parked at the airport?

5 On the return journey Mr Kerr stopped to buy petrol.

a How long did he spend at the petrol station?

b How many more miles did he and his son have to drive to get home?

6 How many minutes did Mr Kerr spend driving his car?

The time graph below shows the flights made by the captain of an aircraft in one day. Design a log book to record the captain's flights. For each flight, record:

- the names of the departure and arrival cities
- the take-off and landing times
- the time spent on the ground at the airport
- the distance flown between each city.

You will need:
- 1 cm squared paper
- ruler

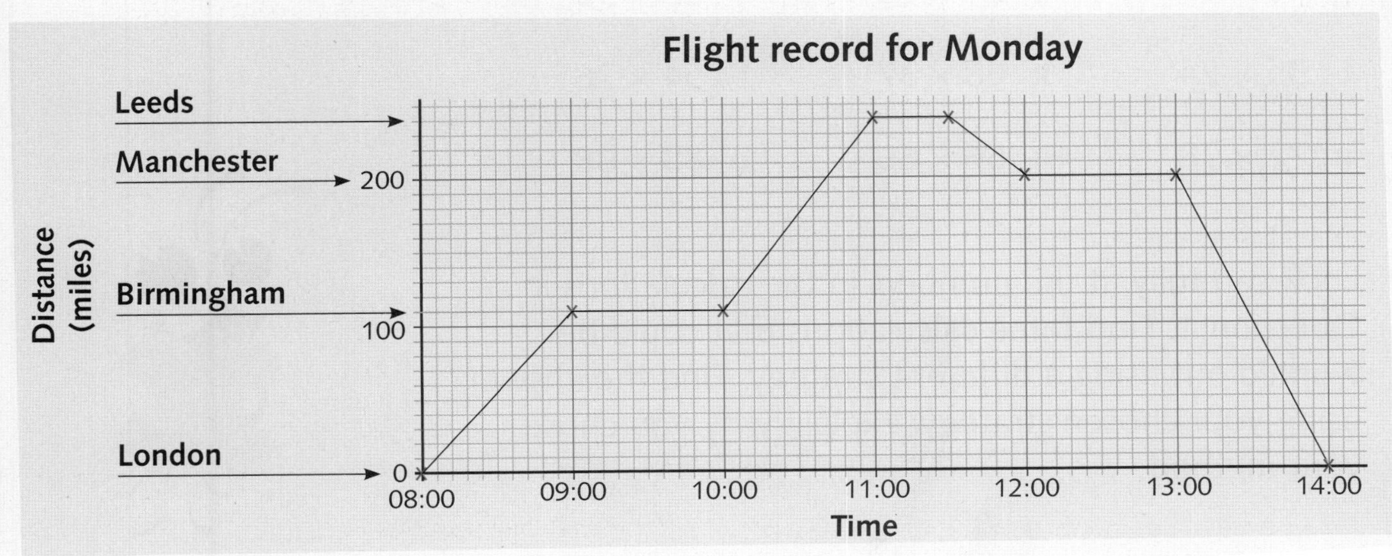

Multiplication TO x TO using partitioning

- Use partitioning to calculate TO × TO
- Estimate and check the answer to a calculation

Challenge 1

1	2	3	4
a 7 × 3	a 6 × 8	a 9 × 4	a 6 × 6
b 70 × 3	b 60 × 8	b 90 × 4	b 6 × 60
c 70 × 30	c 60 × 80	c 90 × 40	c 60 × 60

5	6	7	8
a 8 × 7	a 3 × 8	a 7 × 5	a 9 × 8
b 80 × 7	b 3 × 80	b 70 × 5	b 9 × 80
c 80 × 70	c 30 × 80	c 70 × 50	c 90 × 80

Challenge 2

1 Estimate first then partition each of these calculations to work out the answer.

Example

63 × 38 → 60 × 40 = 2400

63 × 38 = (63 × 30) + (63 × 8)
= 1890 + 504
= 2394

a 46 × 42	b 38 × 33	c 84 × 56
d 48 × 65	e 26 × 39	f 74 × 58
g 78 × 46	h 61 × 78	i 85 × 92
j 35 × 24	k 68 × 37	l 54 × 26
m 72 × 38	n 66 × 66	o 88 × 88

2 Look carefully at the numbers in the calculations in Question 1. Find three calculations that could be worked out using a different strategy. Find the answer using your chosen strategy. Explain why you chose your method.

Challenge 3

1 Using each of the four number cards only once, make a TO x TO calculation that gives an answer as close as possible to the answer shown in the circle.

Example

4 5 3 8 (5000)

$84 \times 53 = (84 \times 50) + (84 \times 3)$
$= 4200 + 252$
$= 4452$

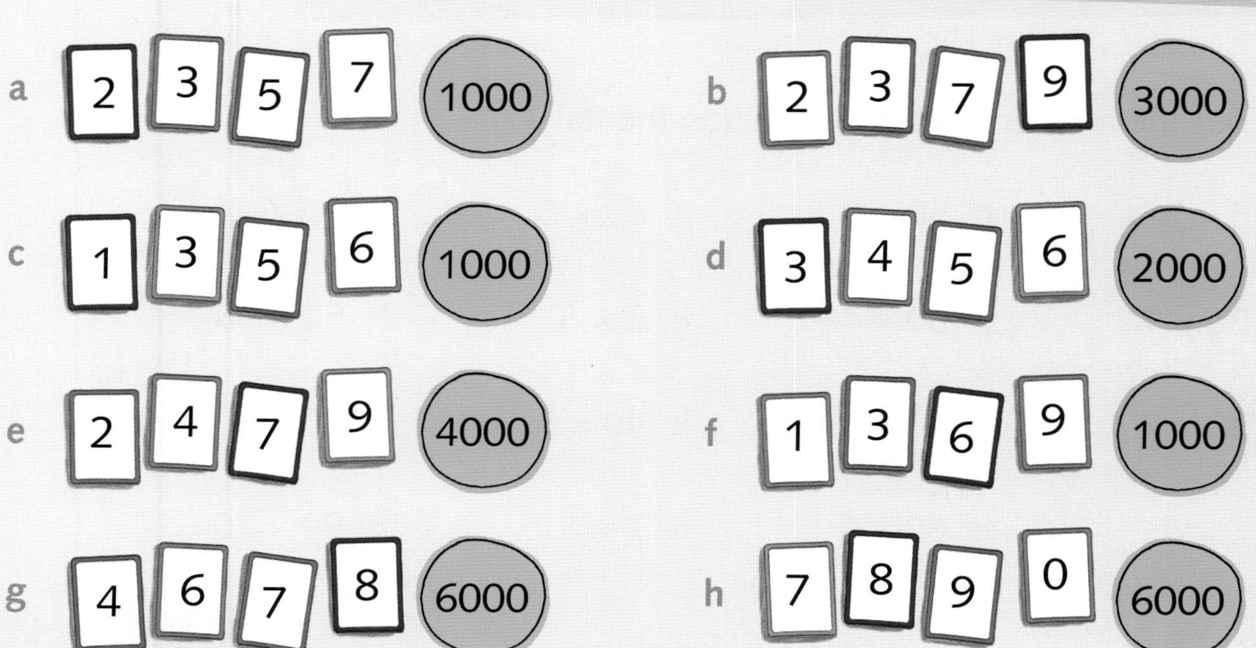

2 Copy these number machines. Write the missing numbers and decide which operations to use.

Hint

An operation may be addition, subtraction, multiplication or division.

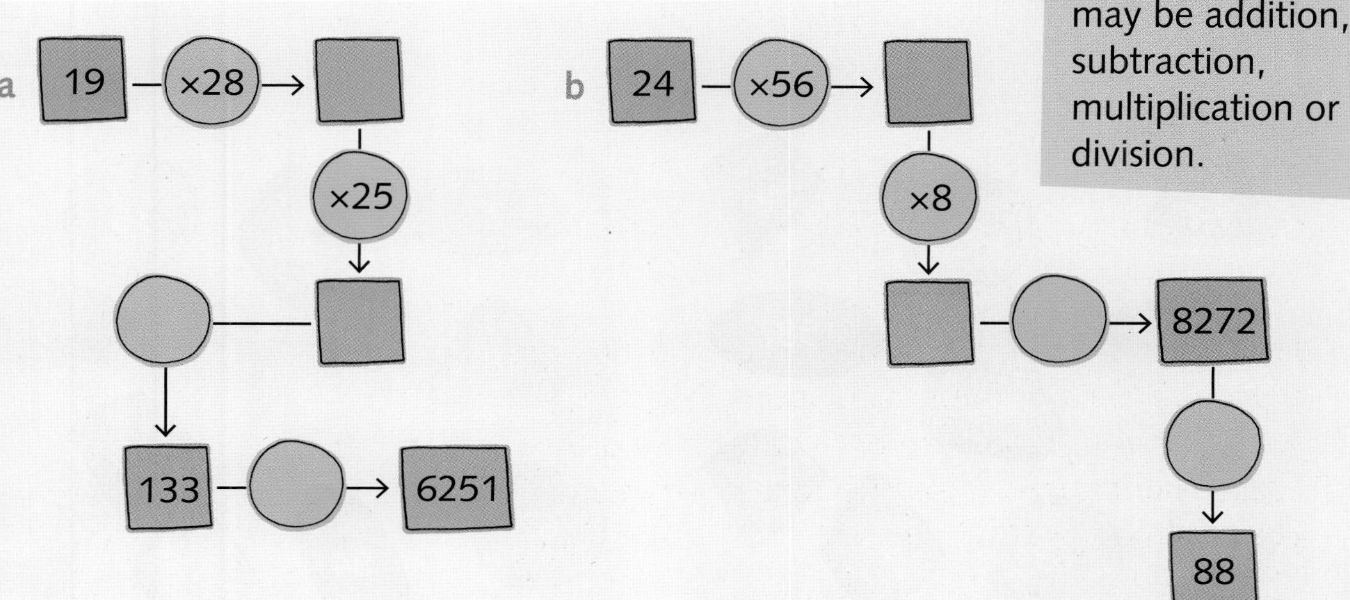

Multiplication TO x TO using partitioning and the grid method

- Use partitioning and the grid method to calculate TO × TO
- Estimate and check the answer to a calculation

Work out the answer to each calculation mentally.

a 6×7	b 50×8	c 60×8	d 9×6
e 80×9	f 80×40	g 3×8	h 50×50
i 30×70	j 40×30	k 40×9	l 70×8
m 7×9	n 60×6	o 7×8	p 90×70

1 Choose a number from each box and create a multiplication calculation. Estimate the answer first. Multiply the numbers together using the grid method. Choose different numbers each time. Write at least eight calculations.

Example

$63 \times 38 \rightarrow 60 \times 40 = 2400$

×	60	3	
30	1800	90	1890
8	480	24	+ 504
			2394
			1

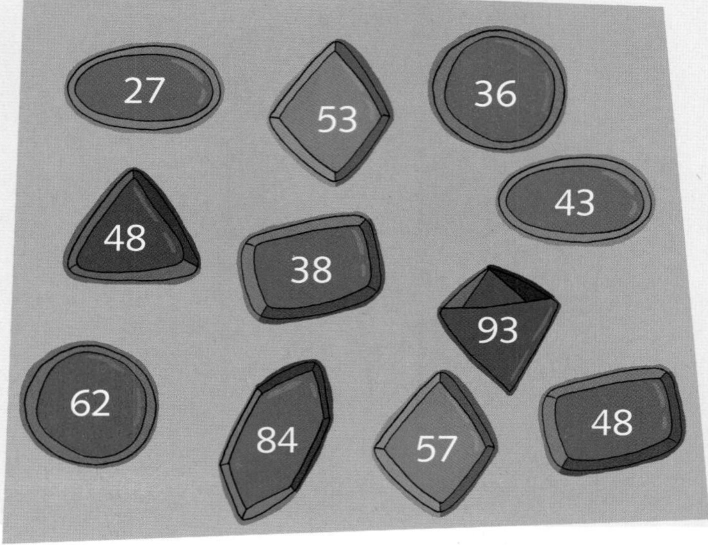

2 Find the answers to these problems about three weeks in a jewellery shop.

> **Hint**
> Use the information in each problem to find the answer to the next problem.

a Week 1: A jeweller has a sales target for sapphire earrings of £2500 for the week. One pair of earrings costs £84. If the jeweller sells 23 pairs of earrings in that week, how close is he to reaching the target?

b Week 2: In Week 2 the sales target is increased by 10%. The jeweller sells 15 more pairs of sapphire earrings than the previous week. What is the difference between the target set and the actual sales?

c Week 3: Ruby earrings cost $\frac{1}{3}$ less than sapphire earrings. In Week 3 the jeweller sells the same number of ruby earrings as he sold sapphire earrings in Weeks 1 and 2. How much money is taken on ruby earrings?

1 Find the missing digit or digits in each calculation.

a 19 × 3□ = 665

b 3□ × 18 = 594

c 24 × 6□ = 1632

d 27 × □6 = 1512

e □6 × 58 = 2668

f 3□ × 42 = 1512

g 46 × □5 = 1150

h 39 × □□ = 2145

i 48 × □7 = 2736

j 30 × 5□ = 1530

k 65 × □8 = 1820

l 83 × 3□ = 2905

m 29 × □□ = 1160

n 99 × □□ = 9801

2 Write two different TO × TO calculations that give an answer of:

a 1000 b 816 c 736 d 1650 e 924 f 700

Multiplication TO x TO using the expanded written method

- Use the expanded written method of long multiplication to calculate TO × TO
- Estimate and check the answer to a calculation

For each question, multiply each of the numbers on the yellow leaves by the number on the green leaf at the top.

1 Approximate the answer to each calculation.

Example

63 × 38 → 60 × 40 = 2400

a 46 × 38	b 72 × 39	c 58 × 56
d 64 × 83	e 67 × 49	f 96 × 26
g 88 × 38	h 74 × 68	i 56 × 93

2 Use the expanded written method to work out the answers to the calculations in Question 1. Choose which method is easiest for you.

Example

Th	H	T	O	
		6	3	
×		3	8	
	5	0^2	4	(63 × 8)
1	8	9	0	(63 × 30)
2	3	9	4	
1				

Th	H	T	O	
		6	3	
×		3	8	
1	8	9	0	(63 x 30)
	5	0^2	4	(63 x 8)
2	3	9	4	
1				

Challenge 3

Ali tried to work out the answer to 37 × 24 on his calculator but he found that the 7 key on the calculator was broken. He used these two methods to find his answer:

You will need:
- calculator

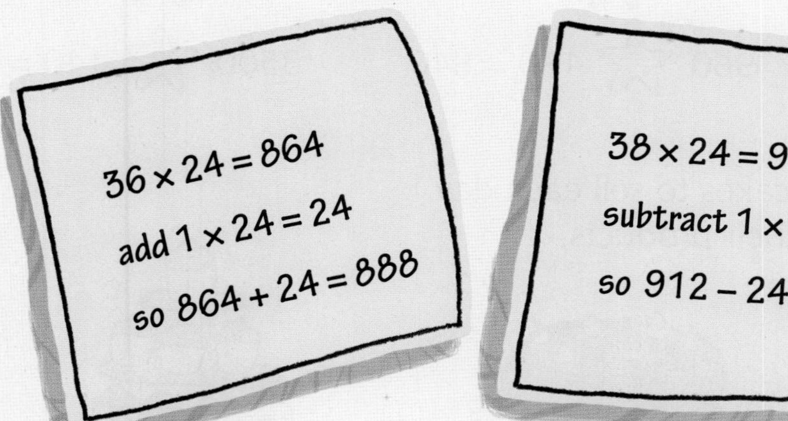

The 7 key is still broken. Explore methods of finding the answer to the following calculations using other keys on the calculator.

Record your methods.

a 67 × 58
b 45 × 27
c 77 × 38
d 73 × 47
e 97 × 57
f 37 × 37
g 77 × 77
h 397 × 965
i 428 × 768
j 647 × 321
k 274 × 83
l 175 × 175

Solving word problems (2)

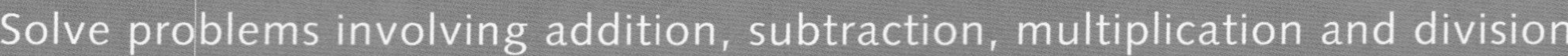

Solve problems involving addition, subtraction, multiplication and division

Challenge 1

Write in the missing operator.

a 4 ☆ 80 = 320
b 640 ☆ 80 = 8
c 110 ☆ 30 = 80
d 600 = 120 ☆ 5
e 70 ☆ 80 = 150
f 120 ☆ 30 = 90
g 7200 = 90 ☆ 80
h 3200 ☆ 80 = 40
i 4800 ☆ 8 = 600
j 1500 ☆ 300 = 5
k 960 ☆ 120 = 840
l 3500 ☆ 140 = 3640

Challenge 2

A bakery produces a variety of cakes to sell each day. Answer these questions about their products.

Baked cheesecake: £23

Chocolate gateau: £36

Cupcake tree: £48

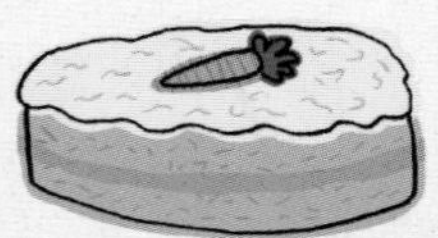

Carrot cake: £29

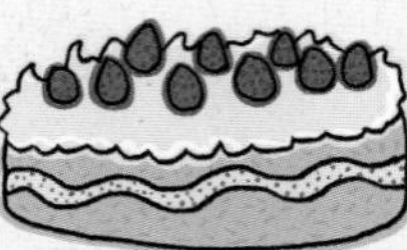

Strawberry gateau: £37

Fruit flan: £25

a The bakery sells 28 chocolate gateaux on Monday. How much money do they take on the sales of chocolate gateau?

b On Friday John is having a party. He buys 15 fruit flans and 26 cupcake trees. How much does he spend?

c The bakery is open 7 days a week. It sells 6 cheesecakes each day. How much money does it take on the sales of cheesecake?

d If you buy 12 carrot cakes and 18 fruit flans, how much change do you receive from £1000?

e Would it cost more to buy 16 cupcake trees or 23 strawberry gateaux? What is the difference in cost?

f If you buy 1 of each product, what is the total cost?

g The bakery has a sale: "Buy 3 get 1 free." Maryam takes home 16 chocolate gateaux. How much does she spend?

h You have a budget of £250 for an afternoon tea party. What would you buy?

i Niall has £130 to spend on carrot cakes. How many cakes can he buy? How much change will Niall receive?

Challenge 3 Find the answers to these problems.

a Janet buys 2 cakes, each at the same price. She pays with a £10 note and gets £2.70 change. What is the cost of 1 cake?

b Jana and William spend the same amount of money at a bakery. William buys 1 large cake for £12. Jana buys 5 cupcakes, which are all the same price, and 1 large cake. The large cake Jana buys costs £6. How much does 1 cupcake cost?

c Sue buys 3 chocolate cookies and 2 coconut macaroons. She spends £3.75 altogether. If the macaroons cost 48p each, how much do the chocolate cookies cost each?

Percentages and hundredths

- Recognise the per cent symbol (%) and understand that per cent relates to 'number of parts per 100'
- Write percentages as a fraction with a denominator of 100

Look at each grid. What fraction and what per cent are shaded blue?

a 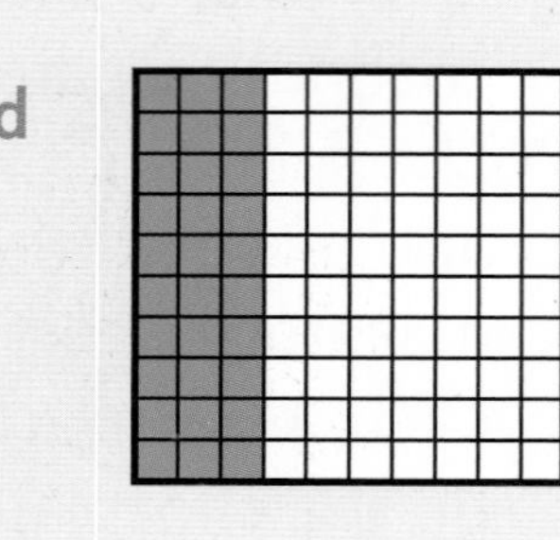

b 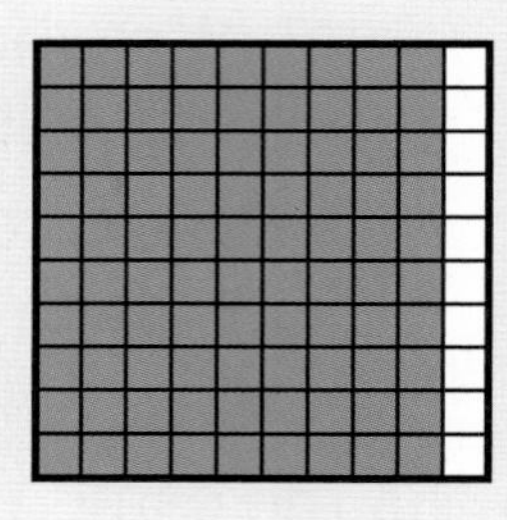

c 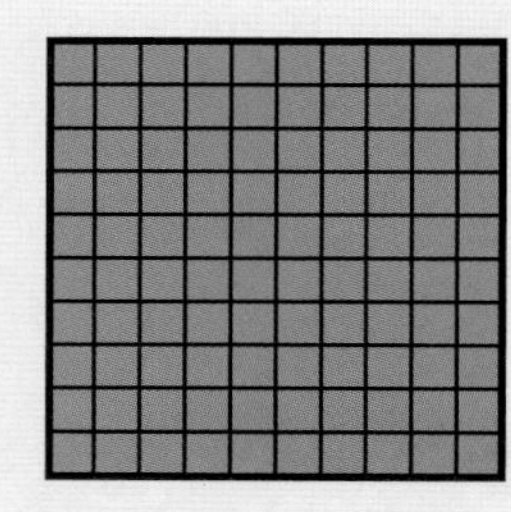

d 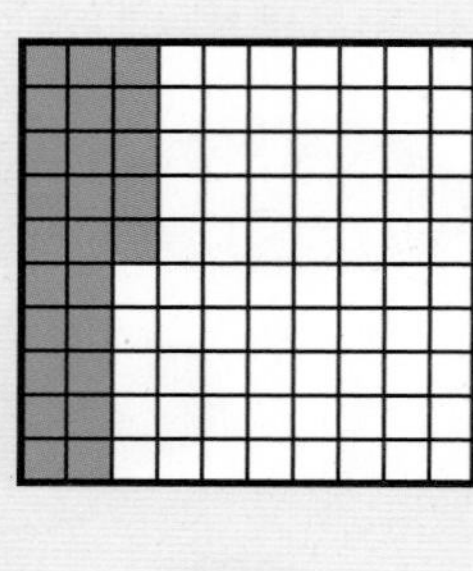

e 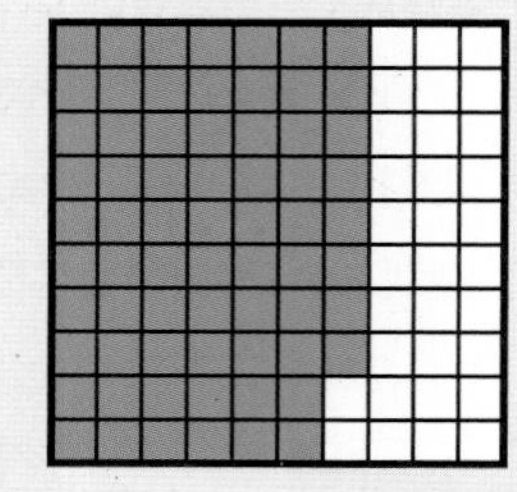

f 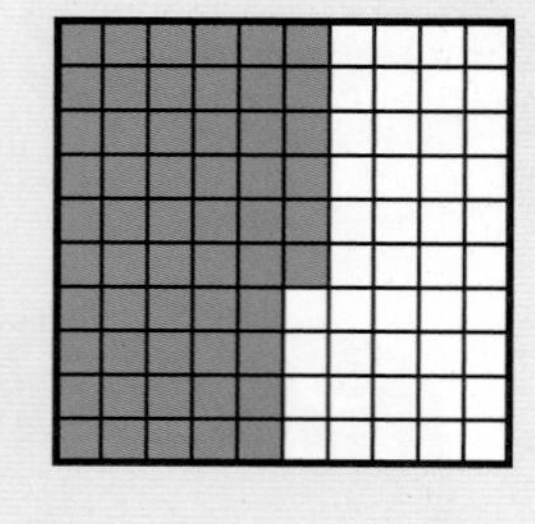

g 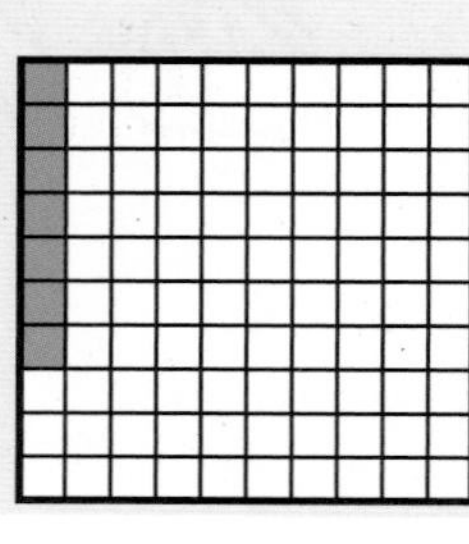

h 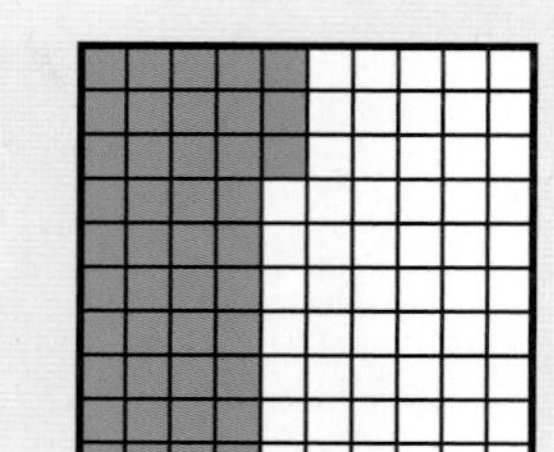

i 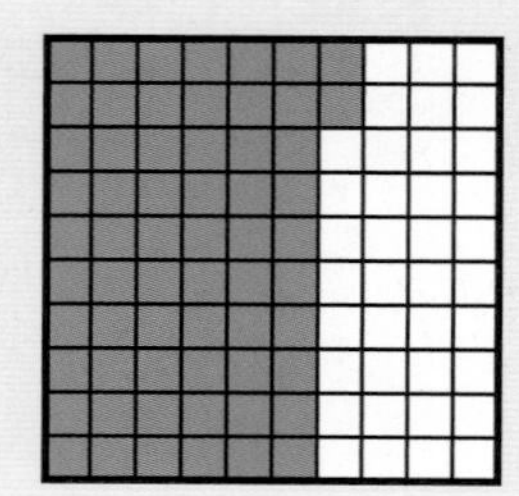

j

k

l

Challenge 2

Play this game with a partner. Use Resource 41: One hundred per cent.

- Resource 41: One hundred per cent
- coloured pencils
- 0–9 dice

- On your own grid choose any five squares to write the letter B in. These are your bonus squares; if you land on them exactly you get an extra turn.
- Take turns to roll the dice. For each number you roll, shade in that many of your squares along the top row and then continue through the grid.
- Say what per cent of your grid is shaded after each turn.
- Your partner says what fraction of your grid is shaded.
- Keep going until one of you reaches 100%. You must be able to colour 100% exactly with your last throw!

1 Explain the connection between hundredths and percentages.

2 Write the equivalent per cent for these fractions.

a $\frac{34}{100}$	b $\frac{59}{100}$	c $\frac{72}{100}$	d $\frac{99}{100}$	e $\frac{1}{100}$
f $\frac{38}{100}$	g $\frac{73}{100}$	h $\frac{1}{2}$	i $\frac{27}{100}$	j $\frac{84}{100}$

3 Write the equivalent fraction for these percentages.

a 12%	b 89%	c 36%	d 3%	e 97%
f 47%	g 100%	h 86%	i 34%	j 3%

Percentages and decimal hundredths

- Recognise the per cent symbol (%) and understand that per cent relates to 'number of parts per 100'
- Write percentages as a decimal to 2 places

Look at each grid. What per cent and what decimal are shaded blue?

Example

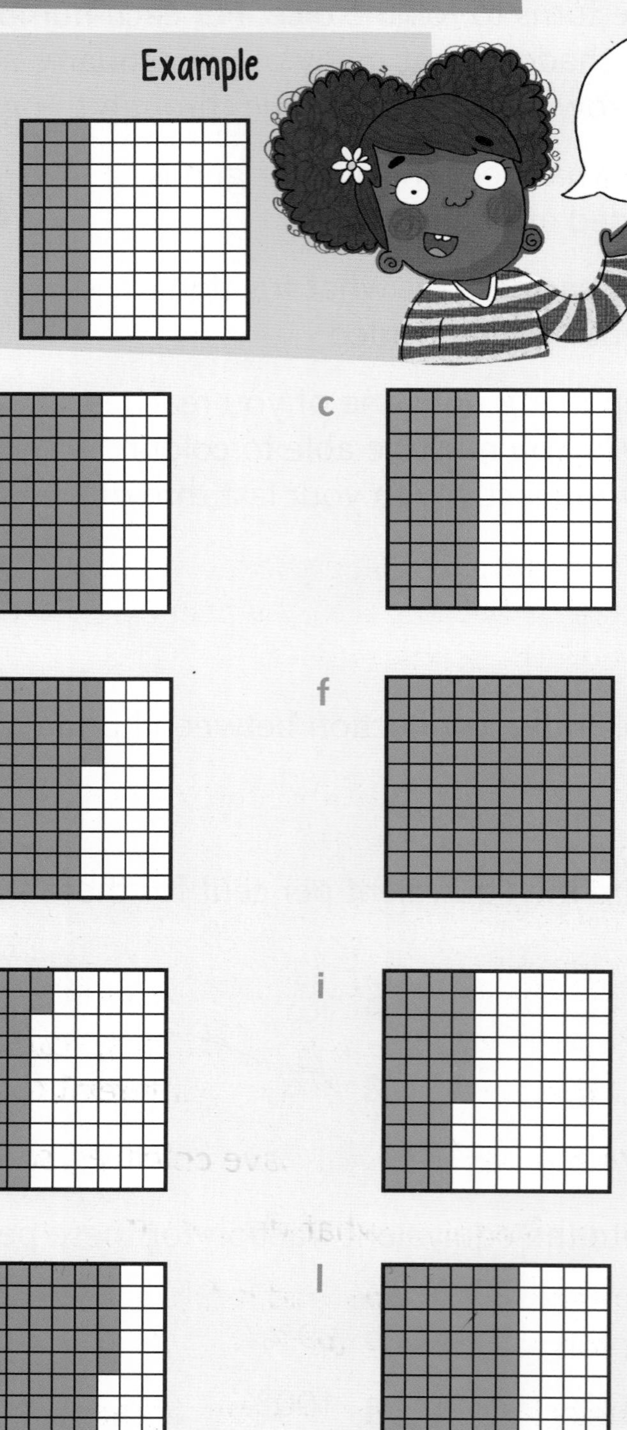

a

b

c

d

e

f

g

h

i

j

k

l

1 Write the equivalent decimal for these percentages.

a 28% b 74% c 15% d 93%

e 6% f 52% g 100% h 39%

0·37 37%

2 Write the equivalent per cent for these decimals.

a 0·72 b 0·81 c 0·17 d 0·96

e 0·55 f 0·39 g 0·04 h 0·22

3 Explain the connection between percentages and decimals to 2 places.

Play this game with a partner. Use Resource 41: One hundred per cent.

You will need:

- Resource 41: One hundred per cent
- Two different coloured pencils (one for each player)
- 1–6 dice

- On the same resource sheet, one player starts from the top of the grid and the other player starts from the bottom of the grid.
- Take turns to roll the dice.
- See what per cent of the grid you can colour in by looking at the table below:

Number rolled	1	2	3	4	5	6
Per cent	8%	9%	11%	15%	1%	5%

- After each roll, colour your squares, starting either at the top or at the bottom. Each use a different coloured pencil.
- Say what per cent you have coloured so far after each go.
- Your partner says what decimal fraction you have shaded so far.
- Keep going until the grid is full. If you cannot colour in the per cent you roll, you miss a turn.

The winner is the player with the highest per cent of the grid coloured in their colour when the grid is full.

Percentages and fraction equivalents

Know percentage equivalents of certain fractions

1 Look at each grid. What tenths fraction and what per cent are shaded blue?

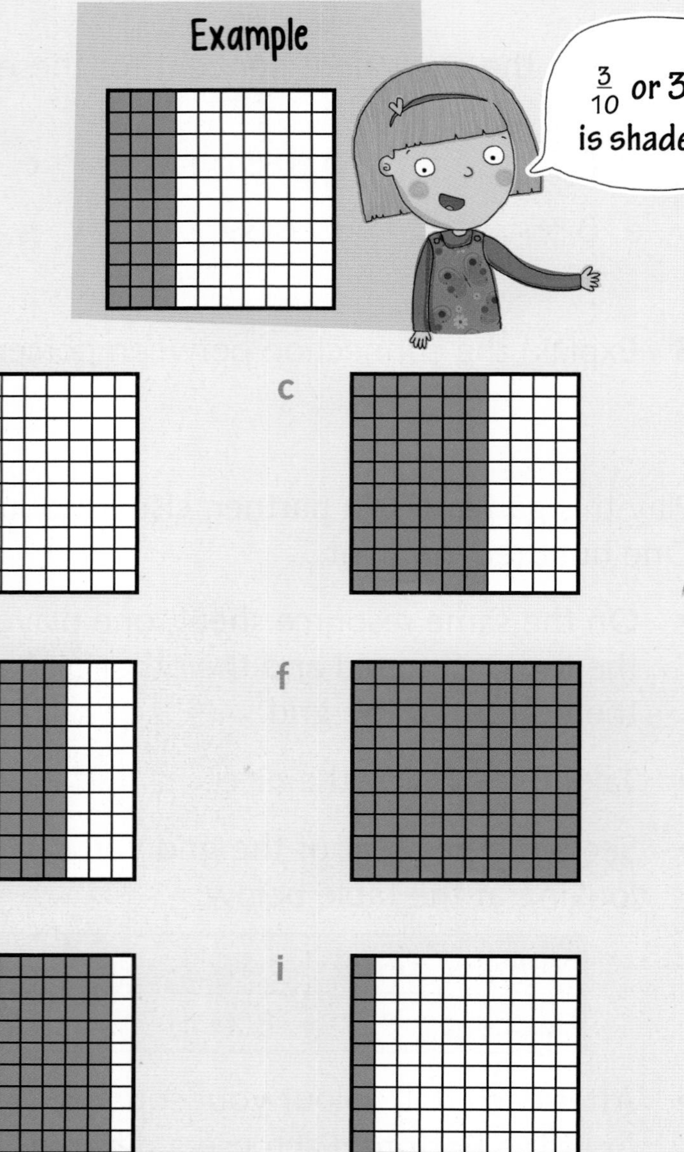

2 Look at Question 1a. What other fraction is it equal to? Explain why this is.

Challenge 2

1 Look at each grid. What fraction and what per cent are shaded blue? Write each fraction as a fifth or quarter fraction.

Example

$\frac{1}{5} = 20\%$

a 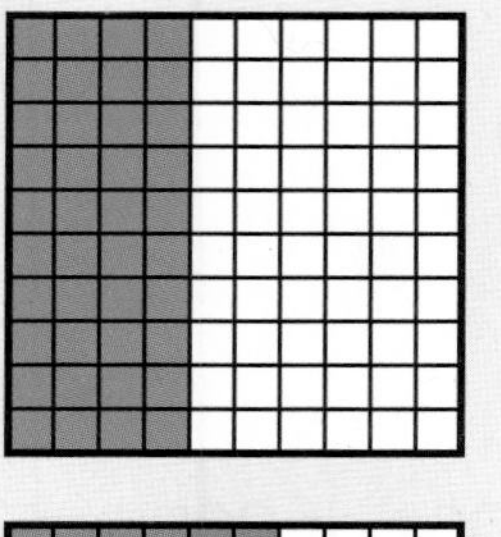

b 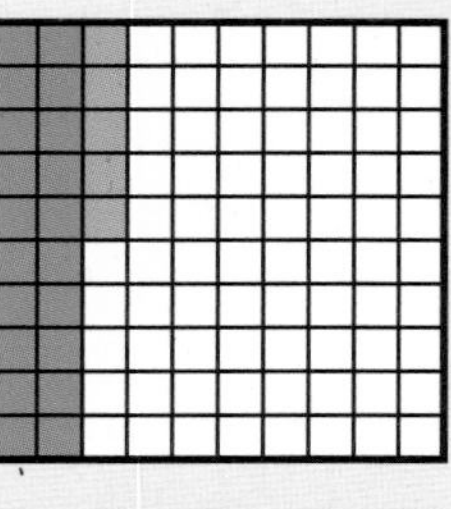

c 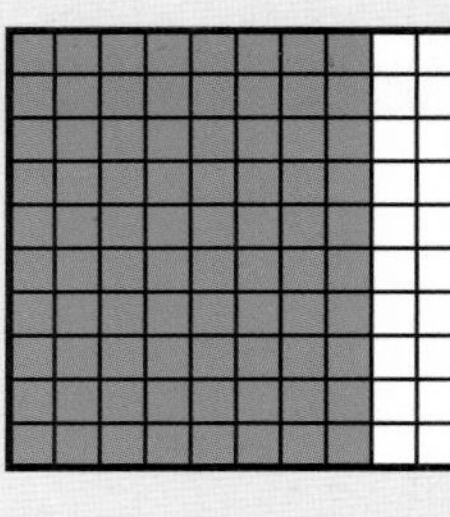

d 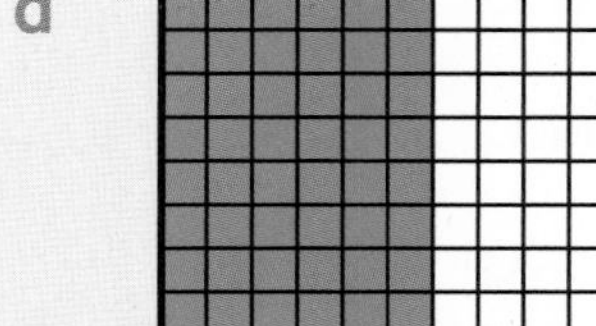

e 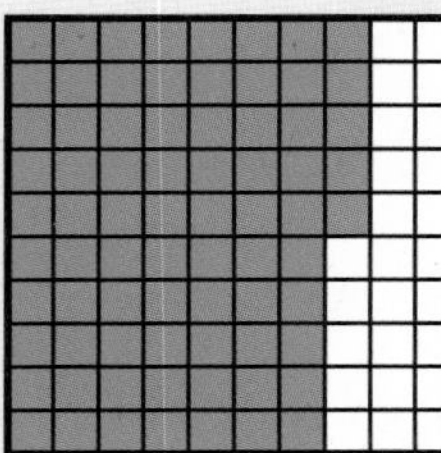

f 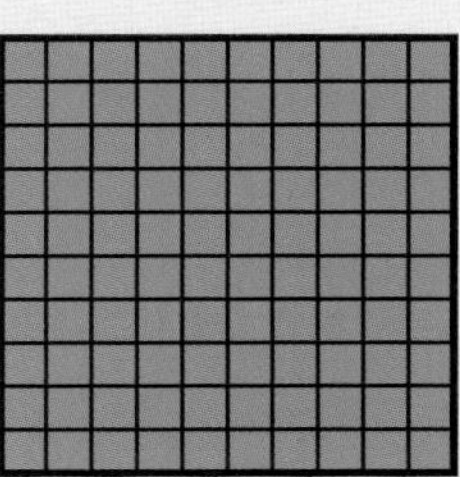

2 Choose a fraction from the first box of fruit and then choose an equivalent percentage and hundredth from the other boxes to match.

Example

$\frac{1}{10} = 10\% = \frac{10}{100}$

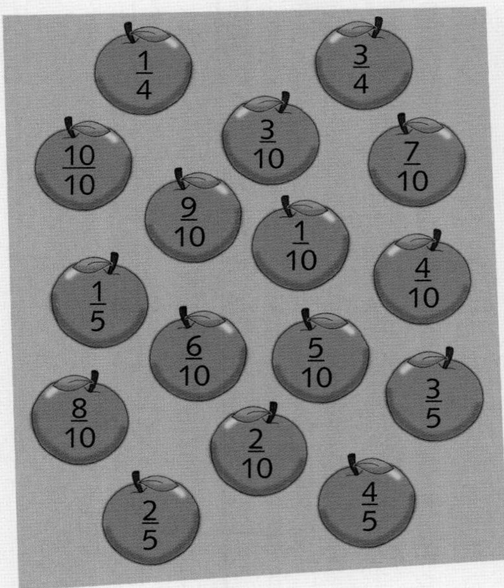

Challenge 3

Design a domino set where equivalent percentages, fractions and decimals are matched.

If you have time, make the dominoes out of card and play the game.

Percentage problems

Solve problems involving percentages

1 Work out these percentages.

a 50% of 300	b 50% of £550	c 50% of 800 km
d 50% of 96 m	e 50% of 640	f 50% of £1660
g 25% of 2600	h 25% of £4000	i 25% of 88 cm
j 25% of 640	k 25% of 1000 m	l 25% of 96 ml
m 10% of £760	n 10% of 2580	o 10% of 530 kg
p 10% of 180 km	q 10% of 3000	r 10% of 330 ml

2 50% of the cake was eaten. What per cent was left?

3 80% of the children in Year 5 walk to school. What per cent do not walk?

4 If Sean got 90% of the questions right in a spelling test, what per cent did he get wrong?

5 In a maths test Samara scored 60 out of 100. What per cent did she get right?

1 Work out these percentages.

a 50% of 3200	b 25% of 4020	c 10% of 3870
d 40% of 2500	e 75% of 6080	f 30% of 5400
g 20% of 7660	h 80% of 5000	i 25% of 5100
j 75% of 4140	k 40% of 2760	l 20% of 6310
m 60% of 7770	n 25% of 4020	o 80% of 5830

2 24% of children have packed lunch. What per cent do not?

3 83% of the children in Year 5 say maths is their favourite subject. How many do not like maths the most?

4 A survey of favourite colours was done. 25% of people said red, 14% said blue, and 35% said pink. What percentage of people asked chose other colours?

5 In a maths test worth a total of 80 marks Mina scored 70%, and in a maths test worth a total of 90 marks Oliver scored 60%. Who answered the most questions correctly?

6 Harry has saved £30. He spends 20% of it on his cinema ticket and 10% of it on popcorn. How much does he have left?

1 One large pizza costs £12.50. If Sophie buys four of them she gets 10% off the total bill. How much would she pay?

2 The tallest person in the class is 160 cm tall and the shortest person is 10% shorter. How tall is the shortest person?

3 Jenna saves £1.75 a week for 16 weeks. She goes shopping and spends 75% of her money on some new shoes. How much does she spend?

4 Computers are usually priced at £215 each. The school has negotiated a deal and can get a 25% discount if they buy 16. What would the price be for 16 computers?

5 My dog has been eating a lot. Last time I took him to the vets he weighed 8 kg. Now he is 20% heavier. What is his new weight? It might help to convert the kg to grams.

6 In Brighton the temperature is 25 °C, but in Edinburgh it is only 80% as hot. What is the temperature in Edinburgh?

7 Joe has a piece of string 220 cm long. He cut off 40% of the string and then cut it into 4 cm lengths. How many 4 cm pieces does he have?

Calculating perimeters

Calculate the perimeter of shapes that can be split into rectangles

Rule

P = 2(*a* + *b*)

You will need:

- ruler

Challenge 1

For each shape:

- Use your ruler to measure in centimetres the sides marked *a* and *b*.
- Calculate the perimeter of the shape using the rule.

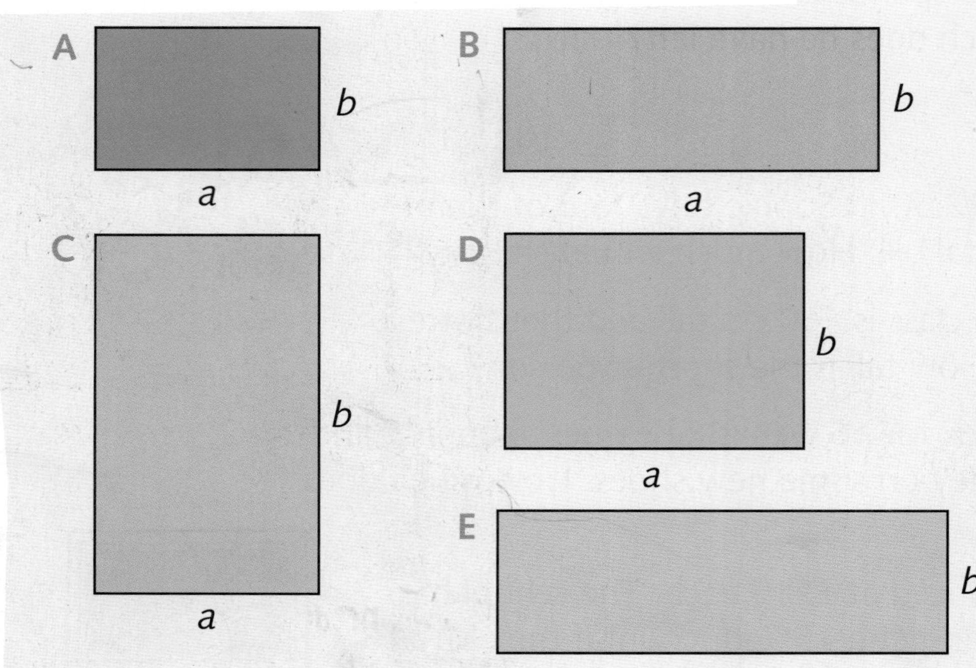

Example

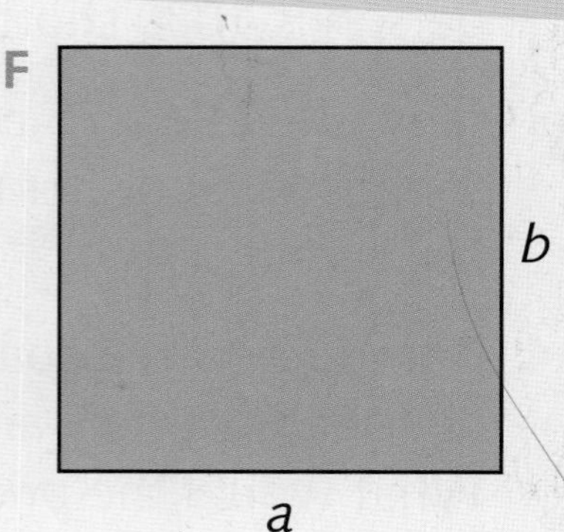

a = 3 cm, *b* = 2 cm
P = 2 × (3 + 2) cm
= 2 × 5 cm
= 10 cm

Challenge 2

1 Calculate the perimeter of each shape in centimetres.

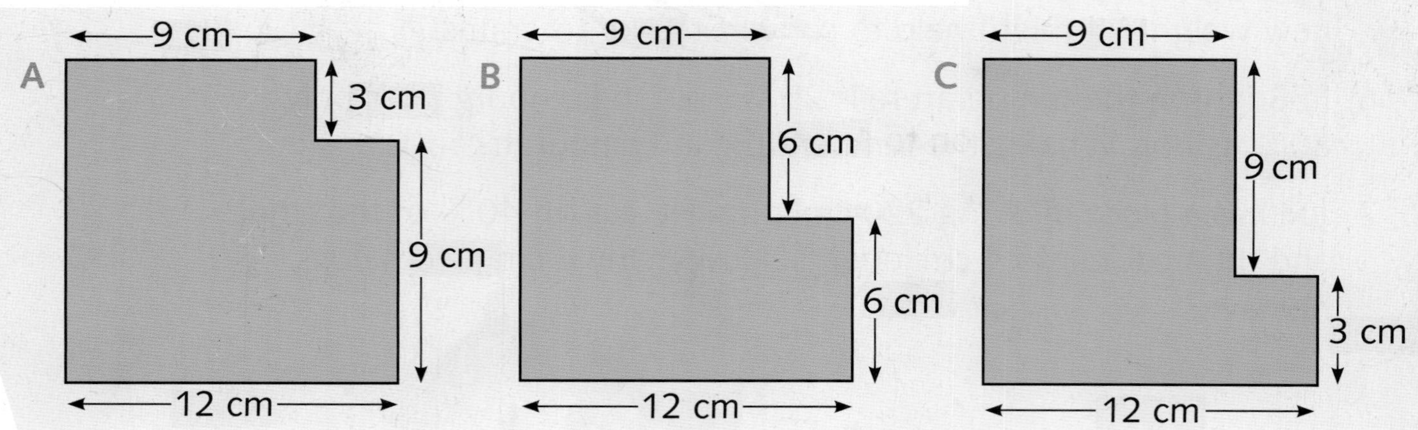

2 These shapes are made by joining the same green and yellow rectangles in different ways. Find the perimeter of each shape in centimetres.

3 Find the perimeter of each swimming pool in metres. Use the dotted lines to help you.

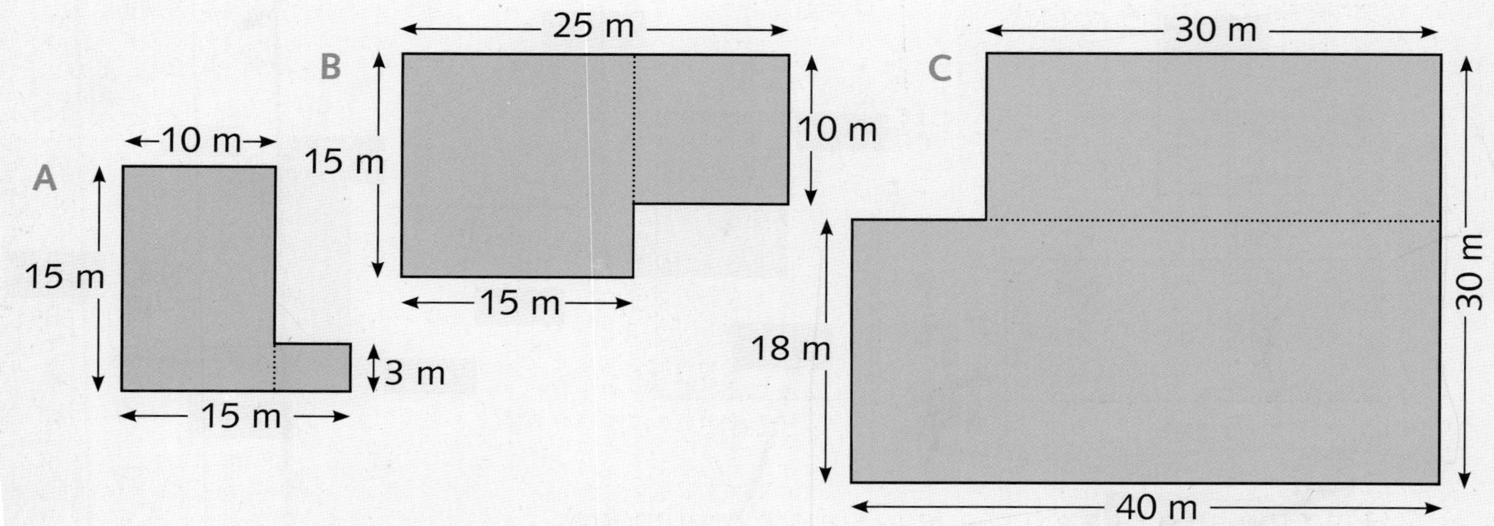

Challenge 3

The pattern of shapes below has been made using regular hexagons with sides of 1 cm.

You will need:
- 1 cm triangular dot paper
- ruler

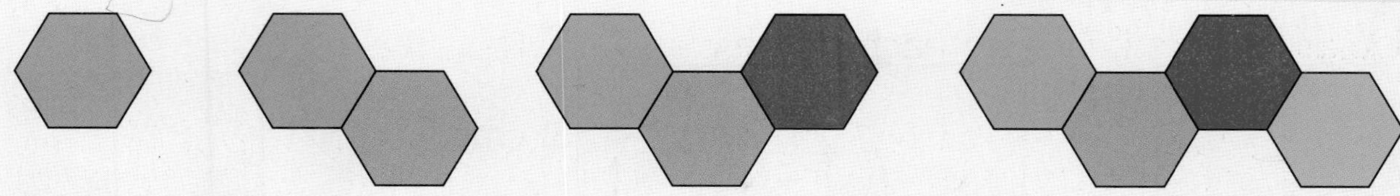

a Copy the four shapes on to 1 cm triangular dot paper.

b Draw the fifth and sixth shapes in the pattern.

c Make a table to record the perimeter for each shape.

d Use your table to predict the perimeter of the tenth shape in the pattern.

Using square units

Calculate the area of rectangles, in square centimetres and square metres, using the rule A = $a \times b$

You will need:

- 1 cm squared paper
- ruler

Rule

A = $a \times b$

Challenge 1

1 Draw these shapes on 1 cm squared paper.

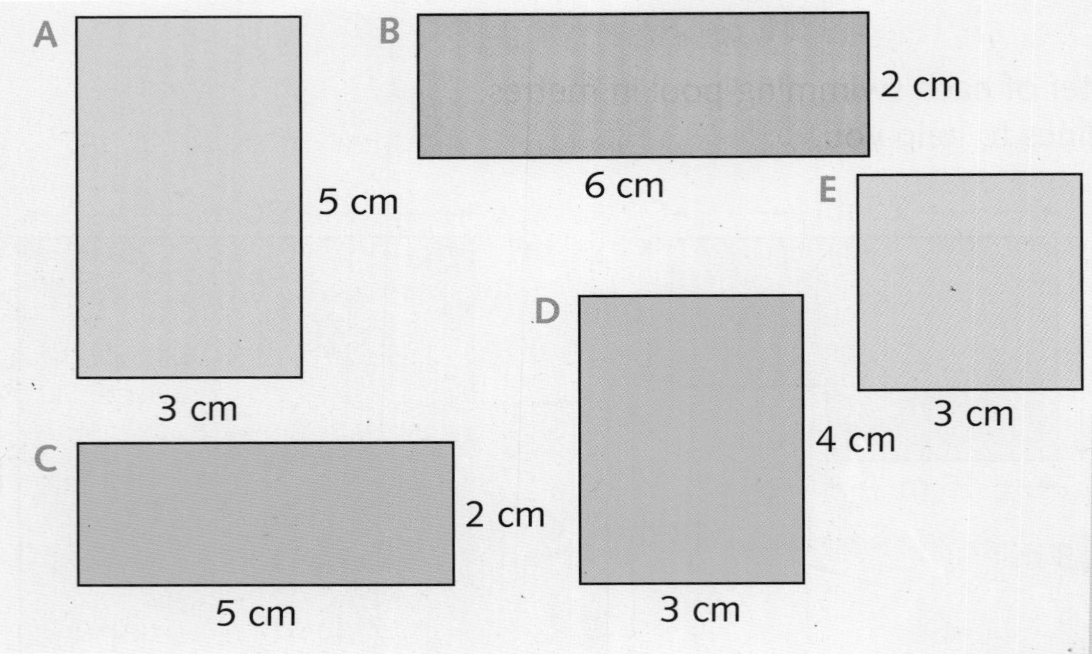

Example

A = 4 cm x 2 cm
= 8 cm^2

2 Find the area of each shape in square centimetres.

Challenge 2

1 Calculate the area of each shape below in square centimetres using the rule.

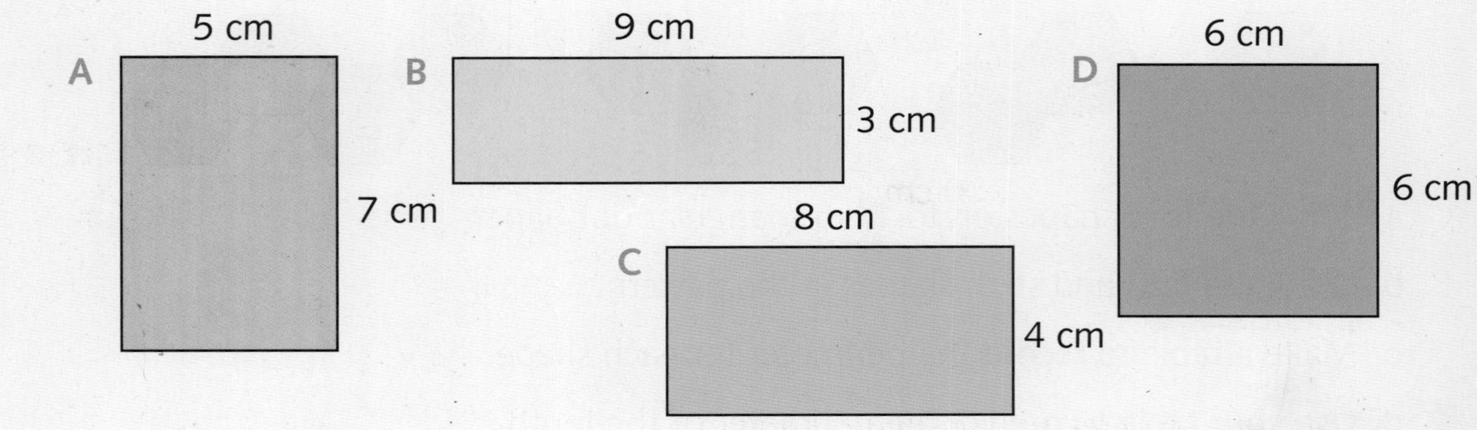

2 Write the four shapes in order of area, largest to smallest.

3 Estimate the area of each of the irregular polygons below in square centimetres. Each small grid square is 1 cm across.

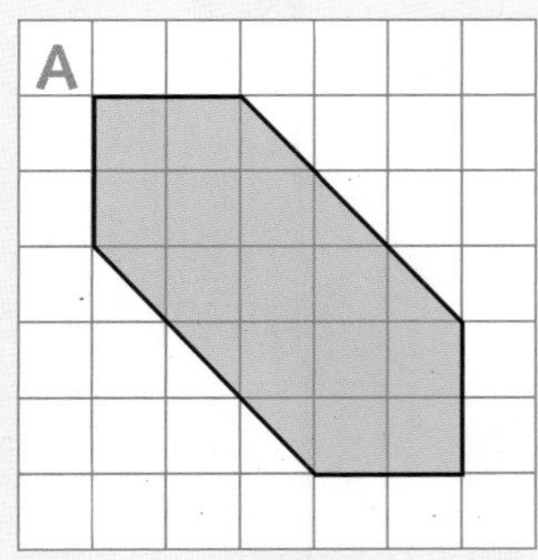

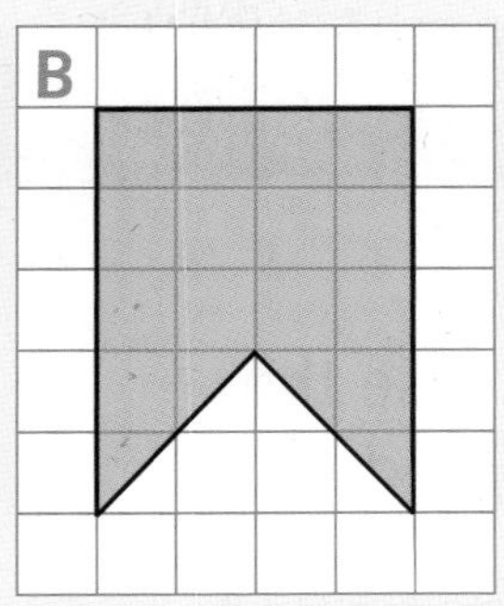

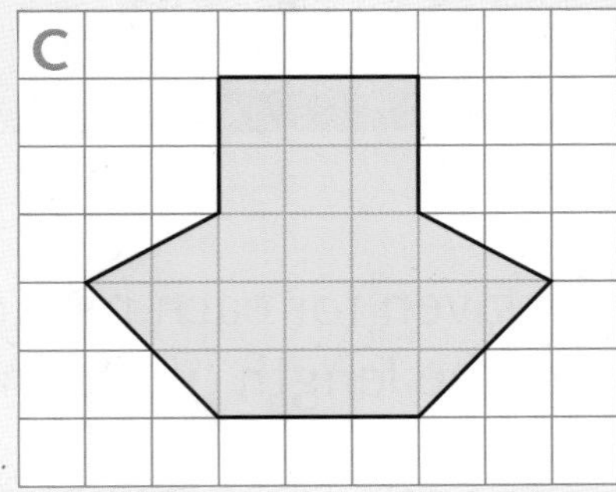

4 Find the area of each of the objects below giving your answer in square units.

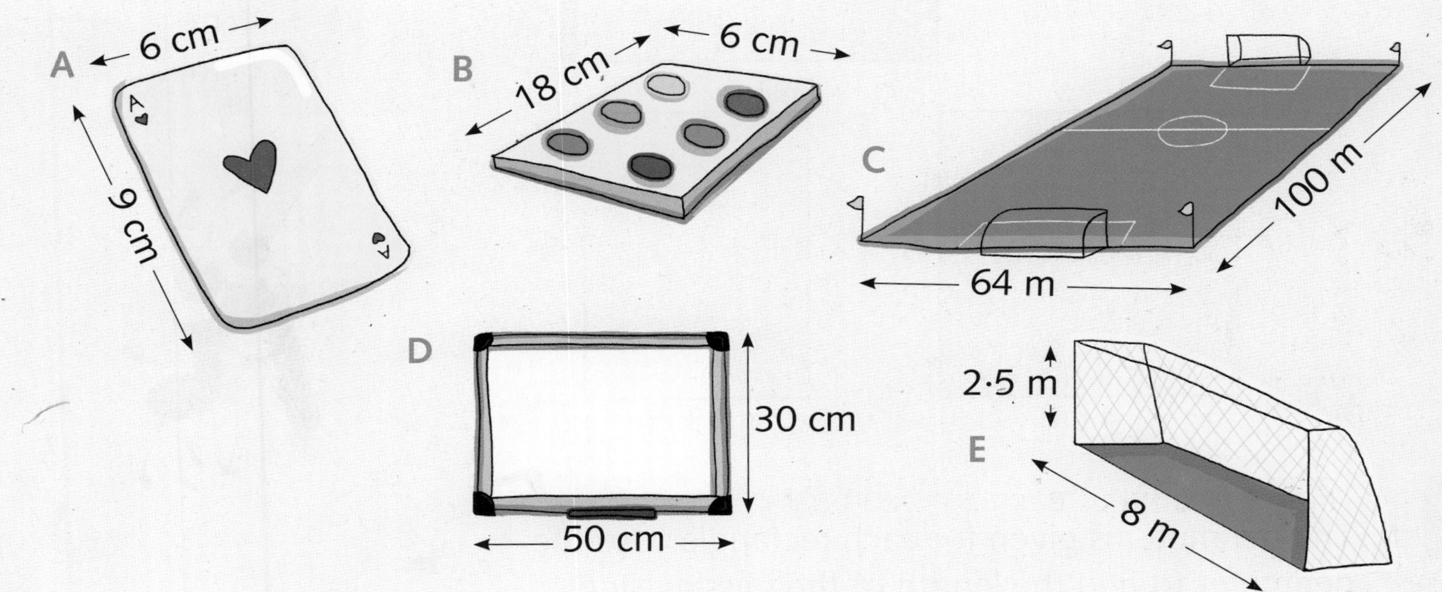

Challenge 3

Each of the windows below has been fitted with square panes of glass.

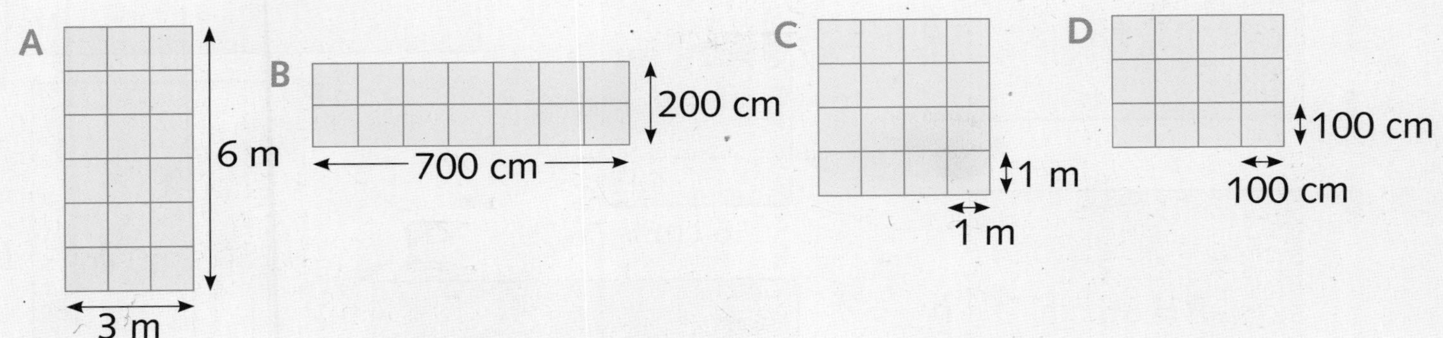

1 Calculate the area of glass in each window.

2 Which window will let in the most light?

Finding missing lengths

Use the relations of perimeter or area to find missing lengths

Challenge 1

The perimeter is given for each rectangle. Use the perimeter to find the length of the missing side.

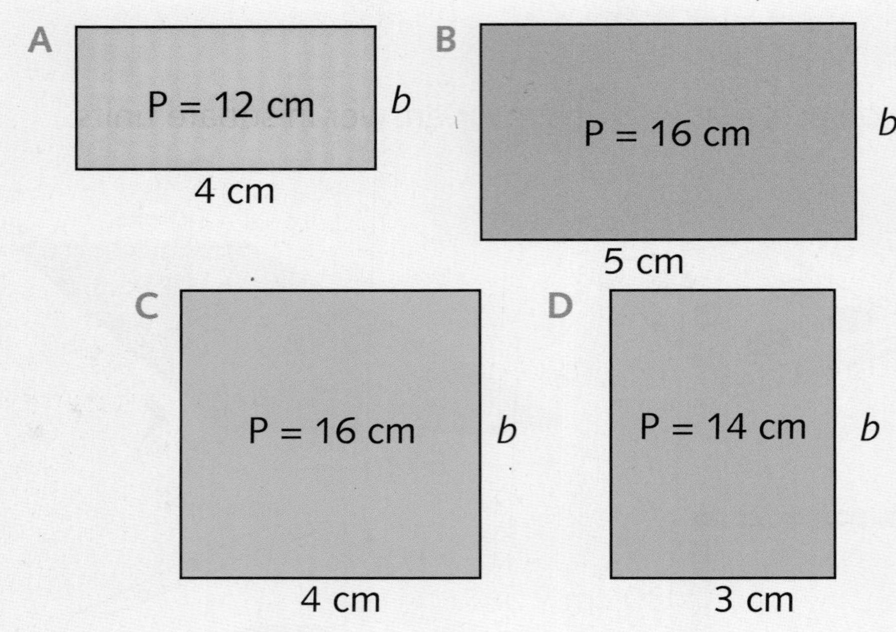

Example

P = 10 cm *b*

3 cm

$P = 10$ cm

$2b = 10 - (2 \times 3)$ cm

$2b = 4$ cm

$b = 2$ cm

Challenge 2

1 The perimeter is given for each rectangle. Use the perimeter to find the length of the missing side.

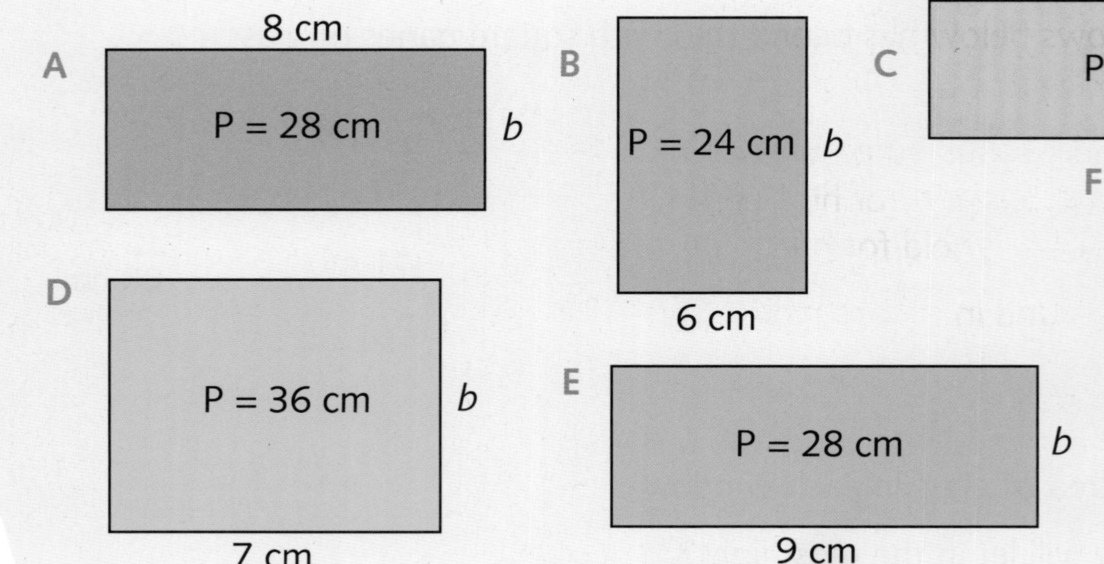

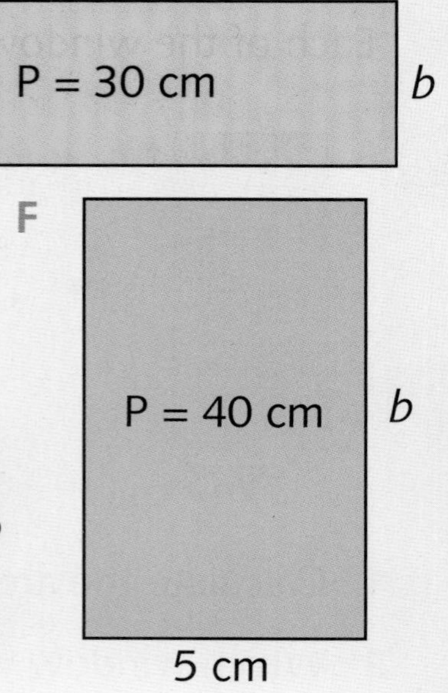

2 The area is given for each rectangle. Use the area to find the length of the missing side.

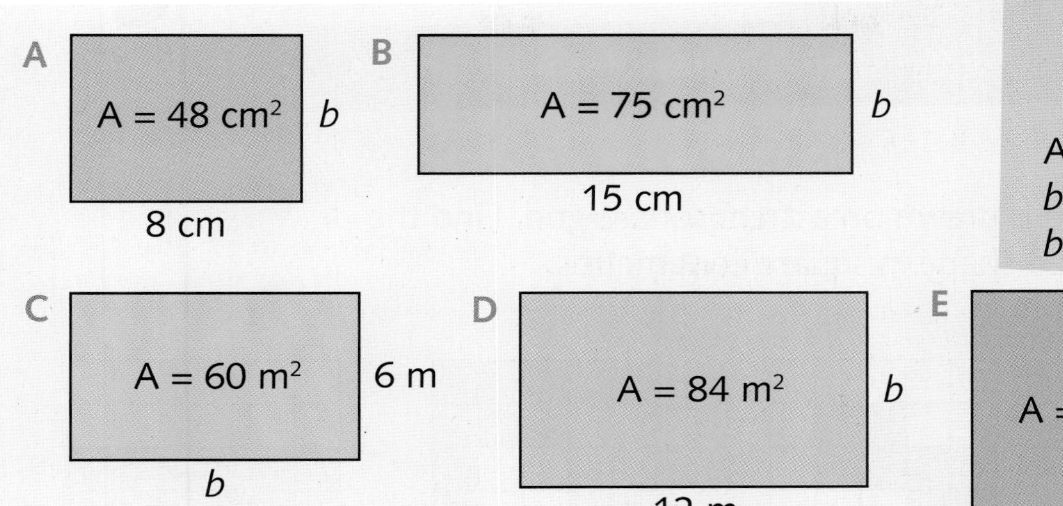

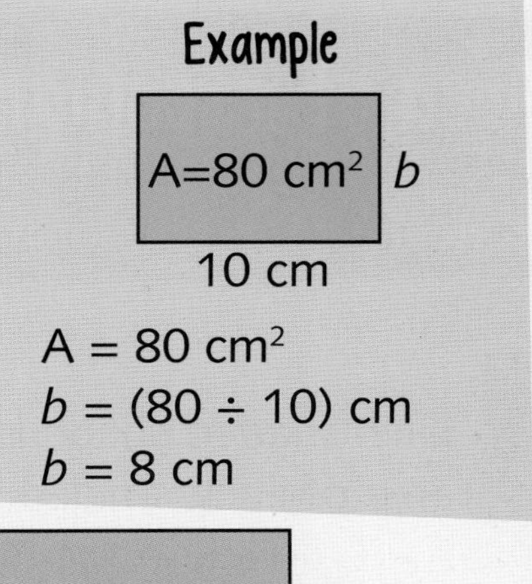

3 Copy and complete each rectangle on 1 cm squared paper.

You will need:
- 1 cm squared paper
- ruler

A

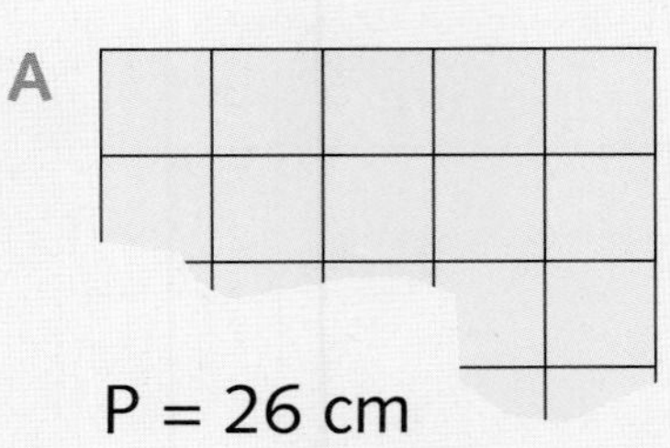

P = 26 cm

B

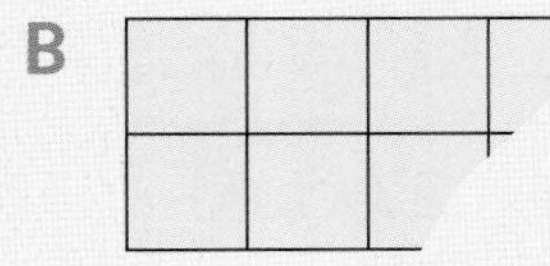

P = 28 cm

a Write down the missing length for each rectangle.

b Calculate the area of each rectangle.

A farmer fences off a rectangular field for his ducks and a rectangular field for his hens. He leaves the rest of the field for his sheep.

Find the area of ground in square metres for:

a ducks b sheep c hens

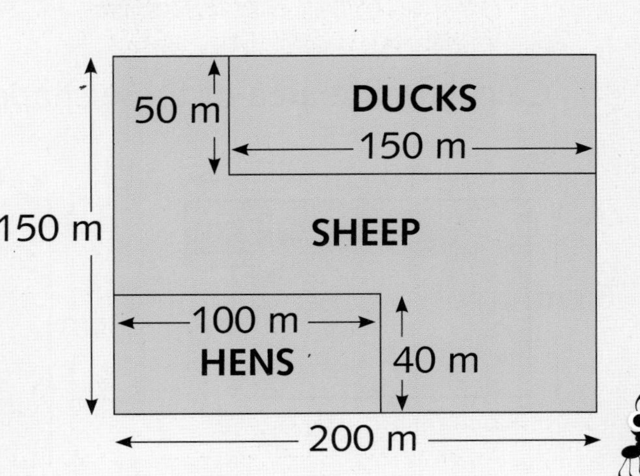

Area of irregular shapes

Calculate the area of irregular shapes formed from rectangles

Challenge 1

Each shaded shape is drawn on a 1 cm square grid. Find the area of each shaded shape in square centimetres.

A
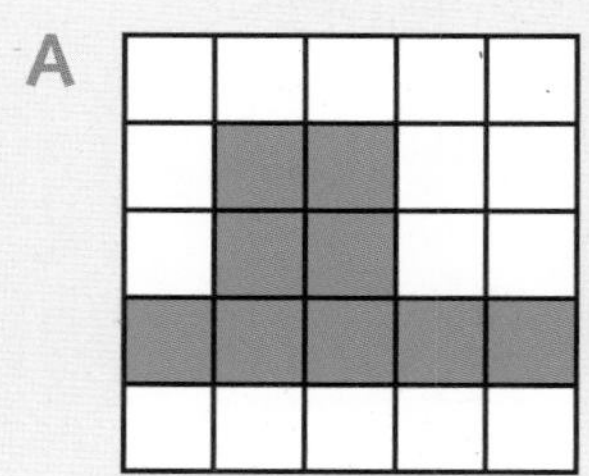

B
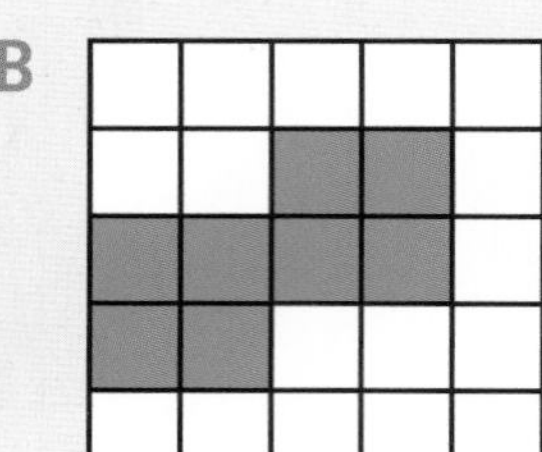

C
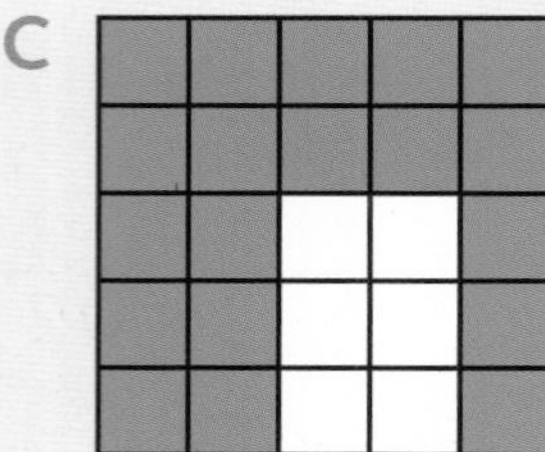

D
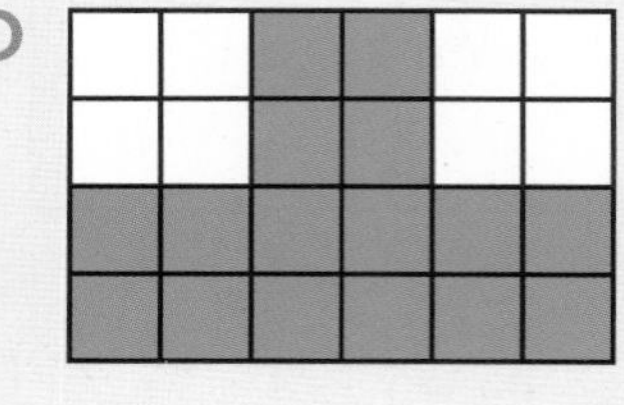

Challenge 2

Rule

You can work out the area of shapes like these by dividing them in three different ways.

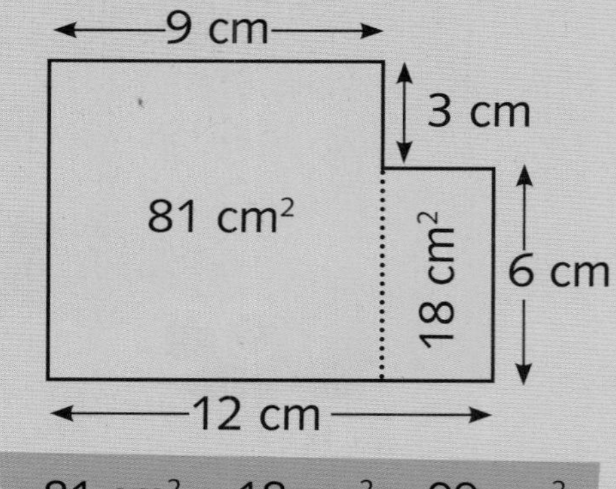

$81\ cm^2 + 18\ cm^2 = 99\ cm^2$

9 cm
27 cm²
3 cm
72 cm²
6 cm
12 cm

$27\ cm^2 + 72\ cm^2 = 99\ cm^2$

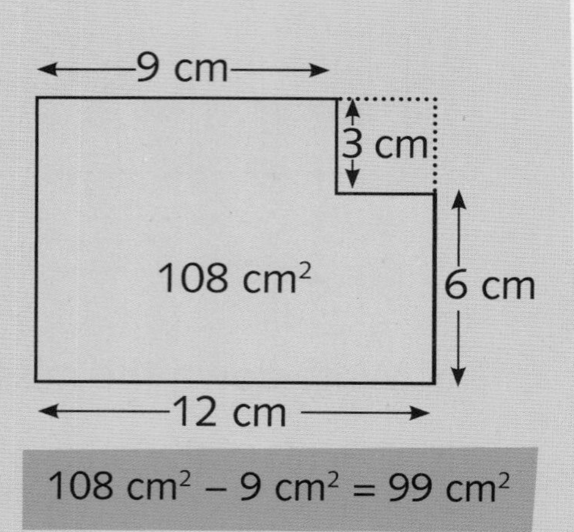

$108\ cm^2 - 9\ cm^2 = 99\ cm^2$

1 Calculate the area of these shapes.

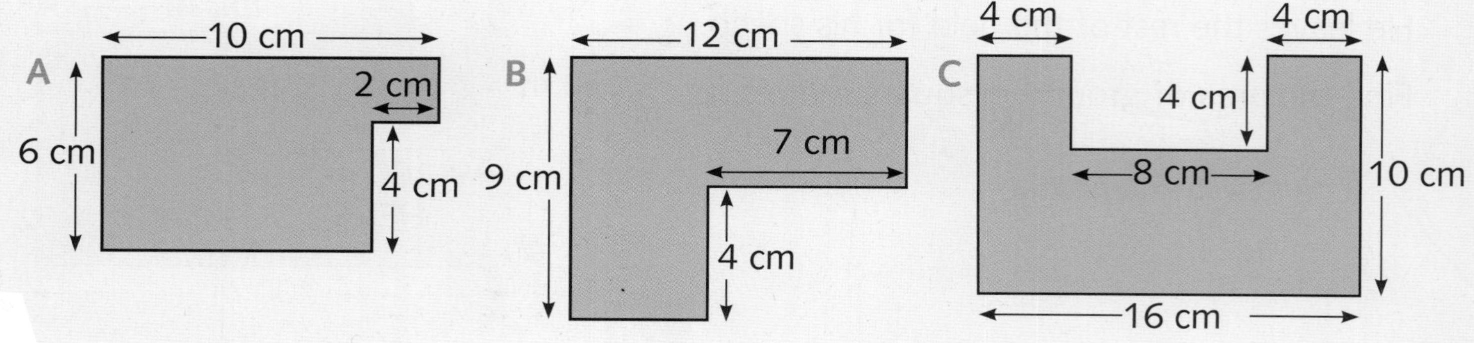

2 Lenny pastes newspaper cuttings about his favourite football team into his scrapbook. Find the area of each of his newspaper cuttings.

A

40 cm
Promotion hopes fade after match
20 cm
20 cm
10 cm

B

30 cm
WE WIN!
20 cm
10 cm
5 cm

C

MATCH UPSET!
10 cm
10 cm
30 cm
25 cm

D

15 cm
Latest signing cheers fans
20 cm
8 cm
5 cm

E

4 cm
9 cm
New stadium plans unveiled
12 cm
16 cm
12 cm

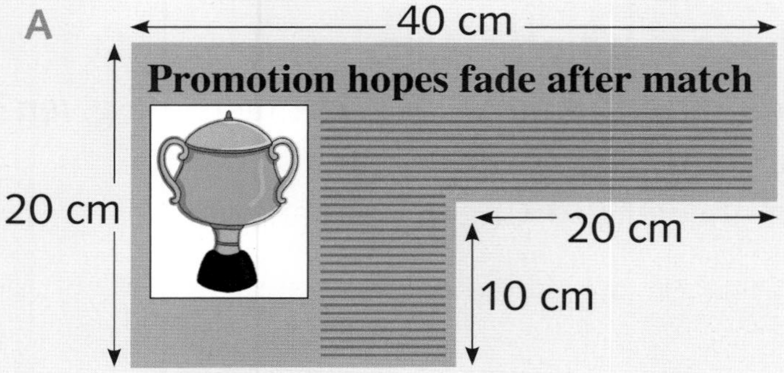

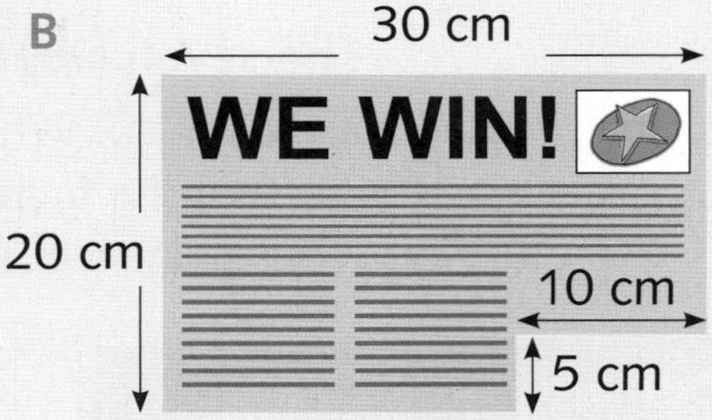

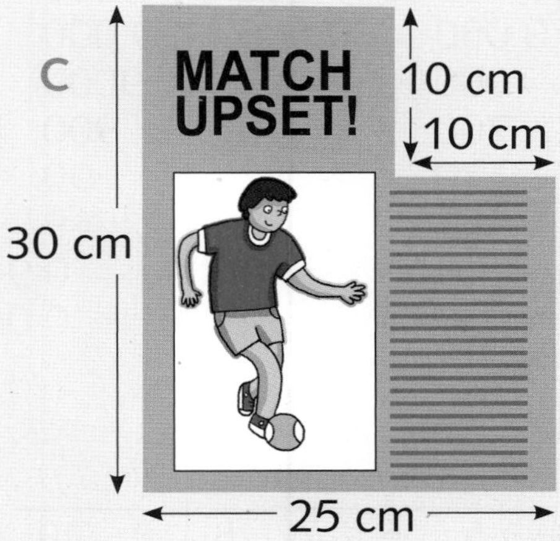

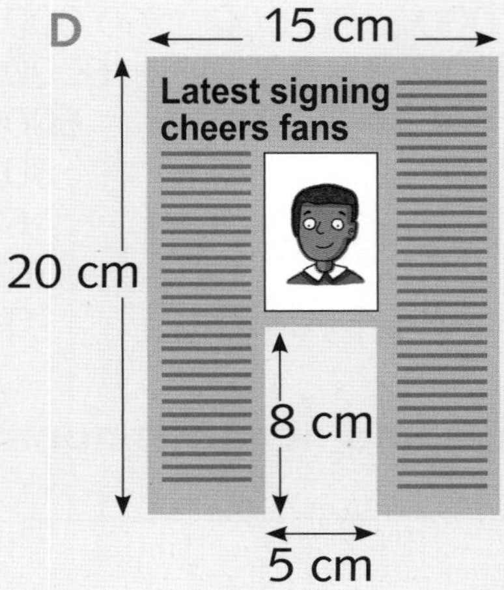

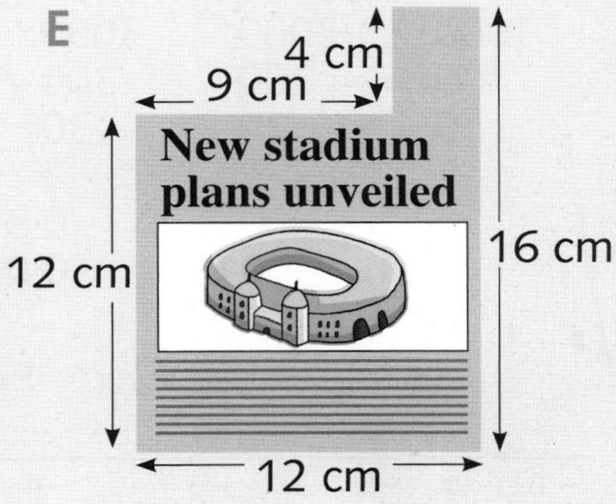

Challenge 3

Each flat shape can be folded up to make a 3-D shape.

- Shape A forms a cube.
- Shape B forms a square-based cuboid.

Use the measurements given to calculate the area of each flat shape.

A

12 cm

B

7 cm
16 cm

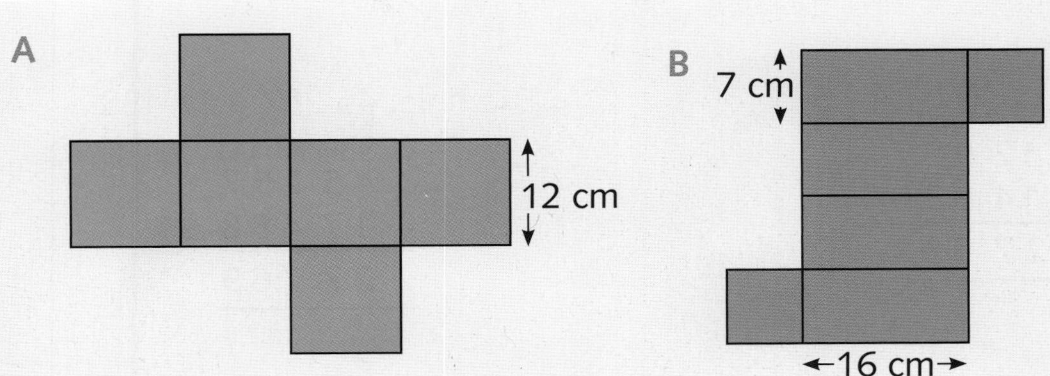

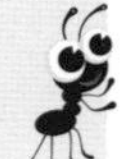

Maths facts

Problem solving

The seven steps to solving word problems

1 Read the problem carefully. 2 What do you have to find? 3 What facts are given?
4 Which of the facts do you need? 5 Make a plan.
6 Carry out your plan to obtain your answer. 7 Check your answer.

Number and place value

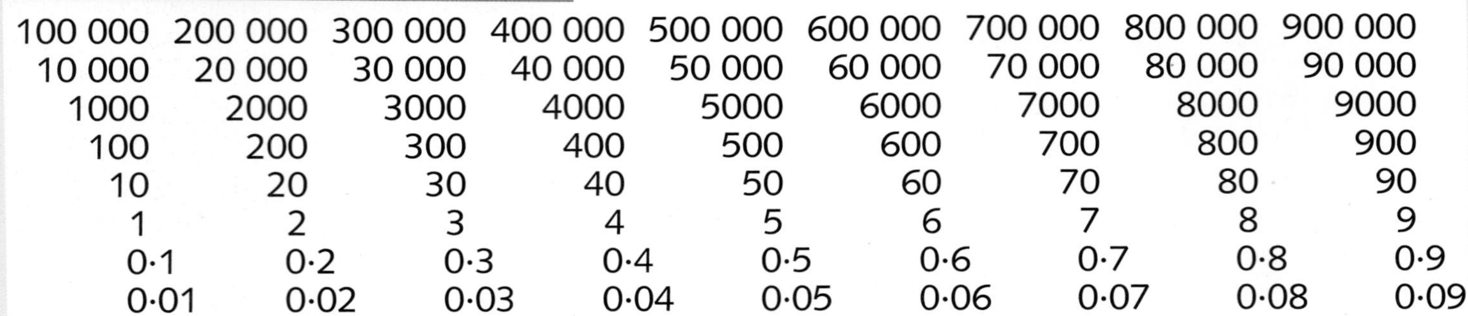

100 000	200 000	300 000	400 000	500 000	600 000	700 000	800 000	900 000
10 000	20 000	30 000	40 000	50 000	60 000	70 000	80 000	90 000
1000	2000	3000	4000	5000	6000	7000	8000	9000
100	200	300	400	500	600	700	800	900
10	20	30	40	50	60	70	80	90
1	2	3	4	5	6	7	8	9
0·1	0·2	0·3	0·4	0·5	0·6	0·7	0·8	0·9
0·01	0·02	0·03	0·04	0·05	0·06	0·07	0·08	0·09

Positive and negative numbers

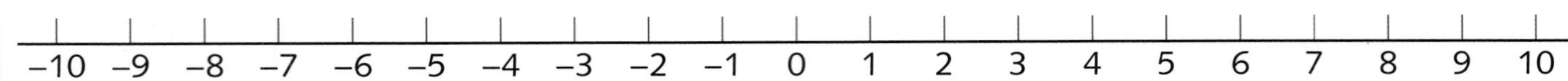

Roman numerals

I	V	X	L	C	D	M
1	5	10	50	100	500	1000

Addition and subtraction

Example: 12 957 + 14 635

```
   12 957
 + 14 635
 --------
   27 592
 --------
    1  1
```

Example: 45 257 – 17 488

```
   3 14  11 14 17
   4̶ 5̶   2̶  5̶  7̶
 –  1 7   4  8  8
 ----------------
    2 7   7  6  9
 ----------------
```

Multiplication and division

Number facts

x	2	3	4	5	6	7	8	9	10	11	12
1	2	3	4	5	6	7	8	9	10	11	12
2	4	6	8	10	12	14	16	18	20	22	24
3	6	9	12	15	18	21	24	27	30	33	36
4	8	12	16	20	24	28	32	36	40	44	48
5	10	15	20	25	30	35	40	45	50	55	60
6	12	18	24	30	36	42	48	54	60	66	72
7	14	21	28	35	42	49	56	63	70	77	84
8	16	24	32	40	48	56	64	72	80	88	96
9	18	27	36	45	54	63	72	81	90	99	108
10	20	30	40	50	60	70	80	90	100	110	120
11	22	33	44	55	66	77	88	99	110	121	132
12	24	36	48	60	72	84	96	108	120	132	144

x	20	30	40	50	60	70	80	90	100	110	120
1	20	30	40	50	60	70	80	90	100	110	120
2	40	60	80	100	120	140	160	180	200	220	240
3	60	90	120	150	180	210	240	270	300	330	360
4	80	120	160	200	240	280	320	360	400	440	480
5	100	150	200	250	300	350	400	450	500	550	600
6	120	180	240	300	360	420	480	540	600	660	720
7	140	210	280	350	420	490	560	630	700	770	840
8	160	240	320	400	480	560	640	720	800	880	960
9	180	270	360	450	540	630	720	810	900	990	1080
10	200	300	400	500	600	700	800	900	1000	1100	1200
11	220	330	440	550	660	770	880	990	1100	1210	1320
12	240	360	480	600	720	840	960	1080	1200	1320	1440

Written methods – short multiplication

Example: 378 x 4

Partitioning

378 x 4 = (300 x 4) + (70 x 4) + (8 x 4)
= 1200 + 280 + 32
= 1512

Grid method

x	300	70	8	
4	1200	280	32	= 1512

Expanded written method

```
   378
 ×   4
    32 (   8 x 4)
   280 (  70 x 4)
  1200 ( 300 x 4)
  1512
   1
```

Formal written method

```
   378
 × 33 4
  1512
```

Written methods – long multiplication

Example: 78 x 34

Partitioning

78 x 34 = (78 x 30) + (78 x 4)
= 2340 + 312
= 2652

Grid method

x	70	8	
30	2100	240	2340
4	280	32	+ 312
			2652

Expanded written method

```
     78
   × 34
  2 3²4 0  (78 x 30)
    3 1³2  ( 78 x 4)
  2 6 5 2
```

or

```
     78
   × 34
    3 1³2  ( 78 x 4)
  2 3²4 0  (78 x 30)
  2 6 5 2
```

Formal written method

```
     78
   × 34
    3 1³2
  2 3²4 0
  2 6 5 2
```

Written methods – short division

Example: 279 ÷ 6

Whole number remainder

$$6\overline{)2\ 7\ ^{3}9}$$ answer: 4 6 r 3

Fraction remainder

$$6\overline{)2\ 7\ ^{3}9}$$ answer: $46\frac{1}{2}$

Decimal remainder

$$6\overline{)2\ 7\ ^{3}9\ .\ ^{3}0}$$ answer: 46·5

Fractions, decimals and percentages

$\frac{1}{100} = 0{\cdot}01 = 1\%$

$\frac{5}{100} = \frac{1}{20} = 0{\cdot}05 = 5\%$

$\frac{25}{100} = \frac{1}{4} = 0{\cdot}25 = 25\%$

$\frac{75}{100} = \frac{3}{4} = 0{\cdot}75 = 75\%$

$\frac{2}{100} = \frac{1}{50} = 0{\cdot}02 = 2\%$

$\frac{10}{100} = \frac{1}{10} = 0{\cdot}1 = 10\%$

$\frac{40}{100} = \frac{2}{5} = 0{\cdot}4 = 40\%$

$\frac{80}{100} = \frac{4}{5} = 0{\cdot}8 = 80\%$

$\frac{4}{100} = \frac{1}{25} = 0{\cdot}04 = 4\%$

$\frac{20}{100} = \frac{1}{5} = 0{\cdot}2 = 20\%$

$\frac{50}{100} = \frac{1}{2} = 0{\cdot}5 = 50\%$

$\frac{100}{100} = \frac{10}{10} = 1 = 100\%$

1 = 100%
$\frac{1}{2}$ = 0·5 = 50% | $\frac{1}{2}$ = 0·5 = 50%
$\frac{1}{3}$ | $\frac{1}{3}$ | $\frac{1}{3}$
$\frac{1}{4}$ = 0·25 = 25% | $\frac{1}{4}$ = 0·25 = 25% | $\frac{1}{4}$ = 0·25 = 25% | $\frac{1}{4}$ = 0·25 = 25%
$\frac{1}{5}$ = 0·2 = 20% | $\frac{1}{5}$ = 0·2 = 20% | $\frac{1}{5}$ = 0·2 = 20% | $\frac{1}{5}$ = 0·2 = 20% | $\frac{1}{5}$ = 0·2 = 20%
$\frac{1}{6}$ | $\frac{1}{6}$ | $\frac{1}{6}$ | $\frac{1}{6}$ | $\frac{1}{6}$ | $\frac{1}{6}$
$\frac{1}{7}$ | $\frac{1}{7}$ | $\frac{1}{7}$ | $\frac{1}{7}$ | $\frac{1}{7}$ | $\frac{1}{7}$ | $\frac{1}{7}$
$\frac{1}{8}$ | $\frac{1}{8}$ | $\frac{1}{8}$ | $\frac{1}{8}$ | $\frac{1}{8}$ | $\frac{1}{8}$ | $\frac{1}{8}$ | $\frac{1}{8}$
$\frac{1}{9}$ | $\frac{1}{9}$ | $\frac{1}{9}$ | $\frac{1}{9}$ | $\frac{1}{9}$ | $\frac{1}{9}$ | $\frac{1}{9}$ | $\frac{1}{9}$ | $\frac{1}{9}$
$\frac{1}{10}$ = 0·1 = 10% | $\frac{1}{10}$ = 0·1 = 10% | $\frac{1}{10}$ = 0·1 = 10% | $\frac{1}{10}$ = 0·1 = 10% | $\frac{1}{10}$ = 0·1 = 10% | $\frac{1}{10}$ = 0·1 = 10% | $\frac{1}{10}$ = 0·1 = 10% | $\frac{1}{10}$ = 0·1 = 10% | $\frac{1}{10}$ = 0·1 = 10% | $\frac{1}{10}$ = 0·1 = 10%

$$\frac{2}{5} + \frac{4}{5} = \frac{6}{5} = 1\frac{1}{5}$$

$$\frac{7}{8} - \frac{3}{8} = \frac{4}{8} = \frac{1}{2}$$

$$\frac{2}{3} \times 4 = \frac{2}{3} \times \frac{4}{1} = \frac{2 \times 4}{3 \times 1} = \frac{8}{3} = 2\frac{2}{3}$$

$$2\frac{3}{4} \times 3 = \frac{11}{4} \times 3 = \frac{11 \times 3}{4 \times 1} = \frac{33}{4} = 8\frac{1}{4}$$

Measurement

Length

1 km = 1000 m = 100 000 cm

0·1 km = 100 m = 10 000 cm = 100 000 mm

0·01 km = 10 m = 1000 cm = 10 000 mm

1 m = 100 cm = 1000 mm

0·1 m = 10 cm = 100 mm

0·01 m = 1 cm = 10 mm

1 cm = 10 mm

0·1 cm = 1 mm

Metric units and imperial units – Length

1 km $\approx \frac{5}{8}$ miles (8 km ≈ 5 miles)

1 inch ≈ 2·5 cm

Perimeter and area

P = perimeter A = area

l = length *b* = breadth

Perimeter of a rectangle

$P = 2(l \times b)$

Perimeter of a square

$P = 4 \times l$

Area of a rectangle

$A = l \times b$

Mass

1 t = 1000 kg 1 kg = 1000 g

0·1 kg = 100g 0·01 kg = 10 g

Capacity

1 litre = 1000 ml

0·1 *l* = 100 ml

0·01 *l* = 10 ml

1 cl = 10 ml

Time

1 millenium	= 1000 years
1 century	= 100 years
1 decade	= 10 years
1 year	= 12 months
	= 365 days
	= 366 days (leap year)
1 week	= 7 days
1 day	= 24 hours
1 minute	= 60 seconds

24-hour time

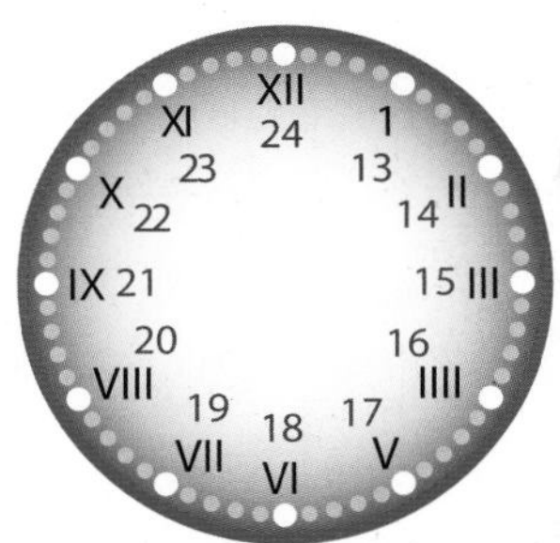

Properties of shape

2-D shapes

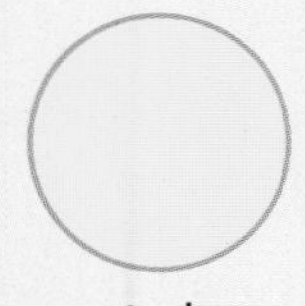
circle

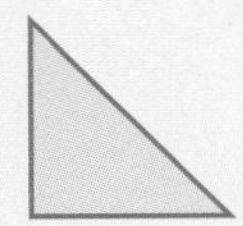
semi-circle

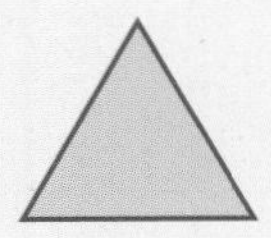
right-angled triangle

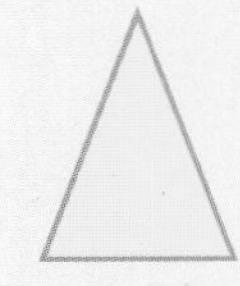
equilateral triangle

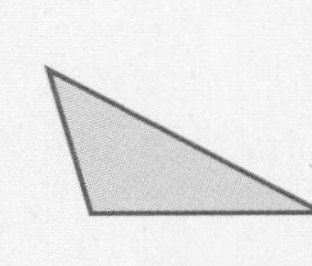
isosceles triangle

scalene triangle

square

rectangle

2-D shapes (continued)

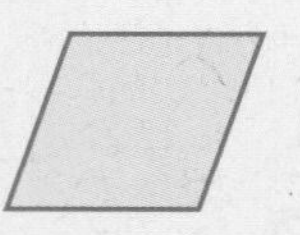
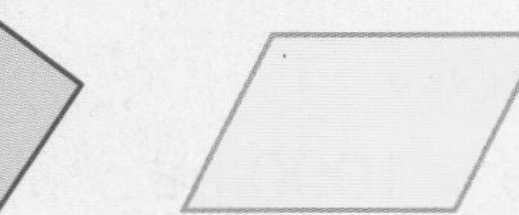
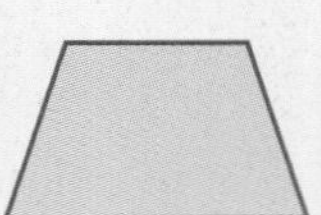
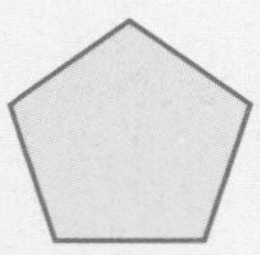
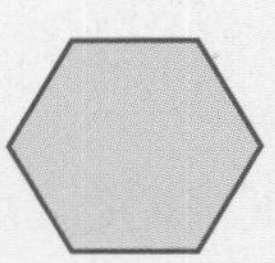
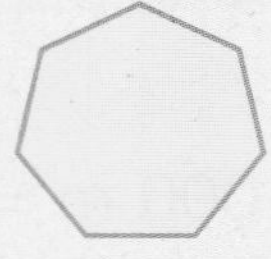
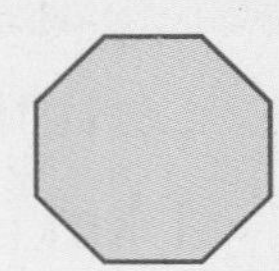

rhombus | kite | parallelogram | trapezium | pentagon | hexagon | heptagon | octagon

3-D shapes

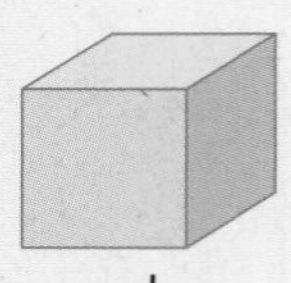
cube

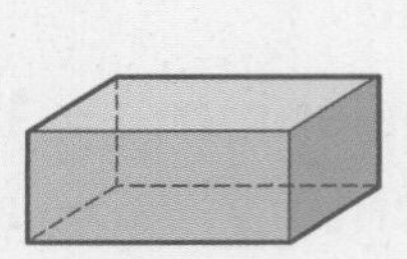
cuboid

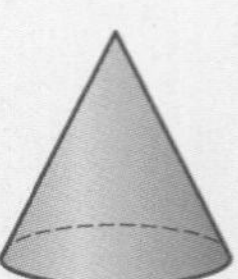
cone

cylinder

sphere

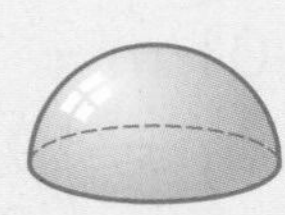
hemi-sphere

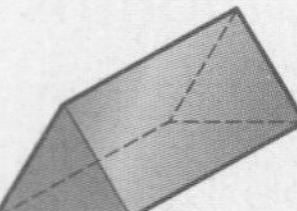
triangular prism

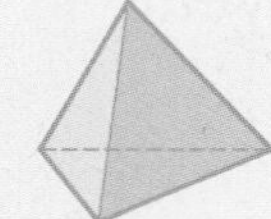
triangular-based pyramid (tetrahedron)

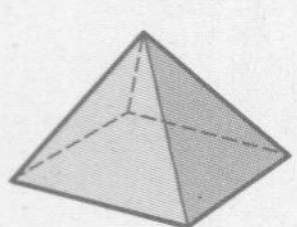
square-based pyramid

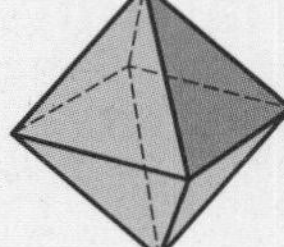
octahedron

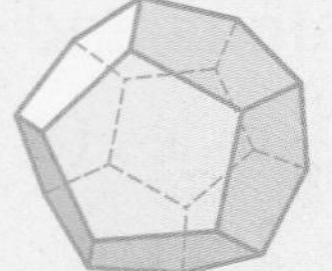
Dodecahedron

Angles

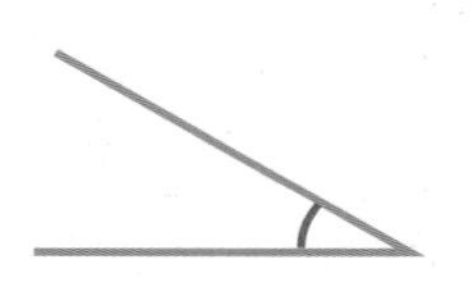
Acute angle
< 90°

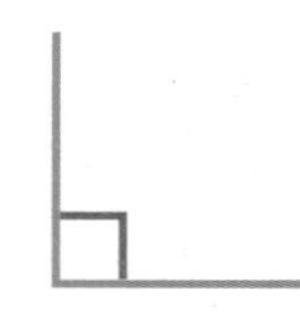
Right angle
($\frac{1}{4}$ turn)
= 90°

Obtuse angle
> 90° and < 180°

Straight line
($\frac{1}{2}$ turn)
= 180°

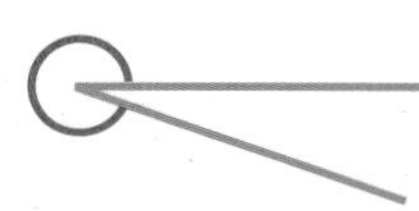
Reflex angle
> 180° and < 360°

Whole turn
= 360°

Position and direction

Coordinates

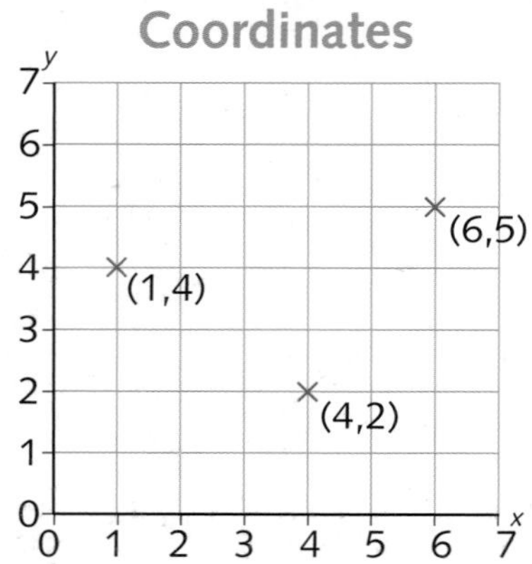

Translation

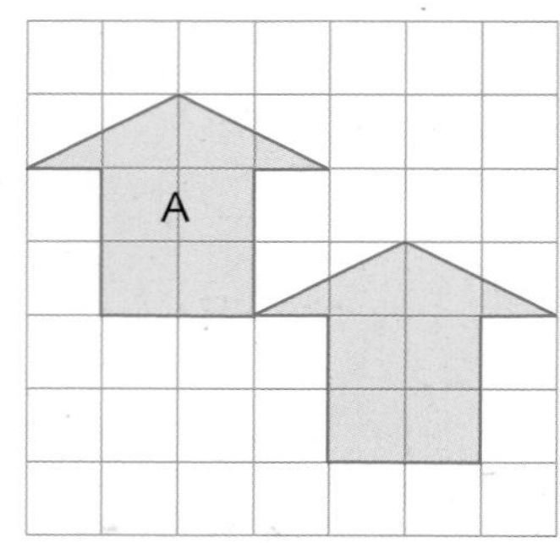

Shape A has been translated 3 squares to the right and 2 squares down.

Reflection

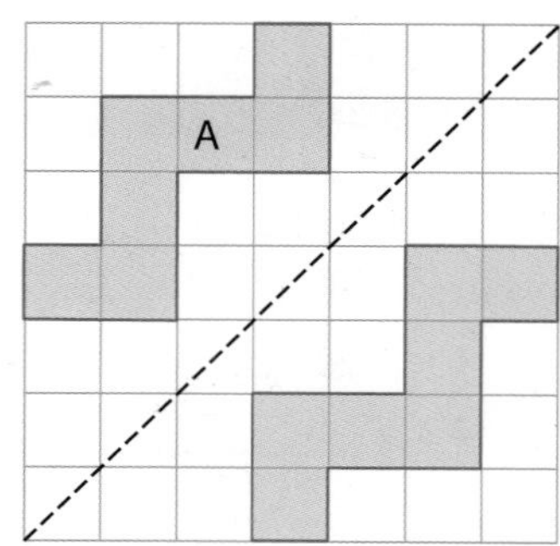

Shape A has been reflected along the diagonal line of symmetry.